goodFOOD

Best Ever
Batch Cooks

First published in Great Britain
in 2026 by Hamlyn, an imprint of
Octopus Publishing Group Ltd
Carmelite House
50 Victoria Embankment
London EC4Y 0DZ
www.octopusbooks.co.uk

An Hachette UK Company
www.hachette.co.uk

The authorized representative in the EEA is Hachette Ireland, 8 Castlecourt Centre, Dublin 15, D15 XTP3, Ireland (email:.info@hbgi.ie)

The recipes in this book have previously appeared on the *Good Food* website.

Distributed in the US by Hachette Book Group, 1290 Avenue of the Americas, 4th and 5th Floors, New York, NY 10104

Distributed in Canada by Canadian Manda Group, 664 Annette St., Toronto, Ontario, Canada M6S 2C8

ISBN: 978-0-600-64032-5
eISBN: 978-0-600-64042-4

A CIP catalogue record for this book is available from the British Library.

Printed and bound in Germany.

10 9 8 7 6 5 4 3 2

Publisher: Kate Fox
Creative Director: Jonathan Christie
Managing Editor: Leanne Bryan
Assistant Editor: Alice Gawthrop
Project Editor: Sarah Reece
Designer: Nicky Collings
Production Controller: Lisa Pinnell

At *Good Food* magazine:
Assistant Publisher: Jennifer Goff
Commercial Director:
Simon Carrington
Food Editor & Test Kitchen Manager:
Ailsa Burt
Group Managing Editor: Lulu Grimes
Art Director: Rachel Bayly
Head of Food: Cassie Best

goodFOOD

Best Ever Batch Cooks

100 FUSS-FREE FREEZABLE & PREP-AHEAD MEALS

hamlyn

Cooks' notes

All the recipes have been triple tested in the Good Food development kitchen and nutritionally analysed by a qualified nutritionist.

Recipes contain nutritional analyses for 'sugar', which means the total sugar content including all natural sugars in the ingredients unless otherwise stated.

Spoon measurements are level unless otherwise specified.

1 teaspoon (tsp) = 5ml

1 tablespoon (tbsp) = 15ml

Both imperial and metric measurements have been given in all recipes. Conversions are approximate and have been rounded up or down. Use one set of measurements only and not a mixture of both.

Wash fresh produce before preparation.

Pepper should be freshly ground black pepper unless otherwise stated.

ICON KEY

✳ *Freezable*

V *Vegetarian*

Ve *Vegan*

Milk should be semi-skimmed, unless otherwise specified.

Eggs should be medium unless otherwise stated. The UK's Food Standards Agency (FSA) advises that raw or lightly cooked hen eggs or foods containing them may be consumed if they have a British Lion mark or are produced under the Laid in Britain egg assurance scheme. This advice does not apply to individuals who are severely immunocompromised and require medically supervised diets prescribed by health professionals. The US Department of Agriculture (USDA) advises everyone against eating raw or undercooked eggs, but in-shell eggs that have been pasteurized may be used safely without cooking.

This book includes dishes made with **nuts** and nut derivatives. It is advisable for customers with known allergic reactions to nuts and nut derivatives and those who may be potentially vulnerable to these allergies, such as babies and children with a family history of allergies, to avoid dishes made with nuts and nut oils. It is also prudent to check the labels of pre-prepared ingredients for the possible inclusion of nut derivatives.

Vegetarians should look for the 'V' symbol on a **cheese** to ensure it is made with a vegetarian rennet.

CONTENTS

Introduction

Busy days are the reality for most of us. Whether it's work, parenting, studying or a combination of all three, time is a limited resource, and when it comes to food, convenience can often take priority over nutrition or taste.

Batch cooking offers a solution. It's a practical, flexible approach to home cooking that helps ensure there's something nourishing, delicious and ready when it's needed most. This book was created to help make that process feel achievable, even for the busiest households. Whether the goal is to save time, reduce stress, eat more home-cooked meals or simply waste less, batch cooking can really help.

And it doesn't mean spending a full weekend cooking for the week ahead. At its heart, it's about planning smarter, not harder – which means choosing to cook something that will store well in the fridge, doubling up the quantities on a favourite dish or stocking the freezer with portions for the week ahead to make everyday cooking quicker and easier.

Why batch cooking works

Batch cooking is built on one simple principle: cook once, eat multiple times. That might mean making extra portions of Tuesday's dinner and freezing them for later, prepping breakfasts ahead to streamline mornings or having go-to soups and sauces ready to reheat. These small changes can make a big difference to how the week flows.

It's also about reducing decision fatigue. When there's already a homemade meal waiting in the freezer or a prepared lunch in the fridge, that's one less thing to think about. And with the rising cost of food, cooking in batches can also help you make the most of ingredients, reduce waste and avoid last-minute takeaways or costly unplanned food shops.

What this book covers

This book has been designed to help batch cooking work across all parts of the day, from breakfasts and snacks to main meals, desserts and bakes. Each chapter focuses on different areas of everyday cooking:

BREAKFAST

Quick, nutritious options to prep in advance and grab on the go. Think make-ahead pancakes, overnight oats and homemade granola.

SNACKS & SHARERS

Light bites to bring out of the freezer when you have people coming round. Choose from treats like cheesy sausage rolls, vegetable gyoza and bake-from-the-freezer pizzas – delicious nibbles designed both to feed a crowd and fill the gap between meals.

SOUPS

Perfect for freezing, soups are one of the easiest meals to batch cook. You'll find classics such as tomato soup and chicken noodle soup, and new favourites, along with storage tips.

MEAT, CHICKEN & FISH

These chapters cover satisfying mains that freeze well or generate enough leftovers to last a few days, from chillies, curries and cottage pie to meatballs, slow-cooked stews and pasta bakes.

VEG

Delicious plant-based mains, from one-pot pasta sauces and veggie pies to make-ahead tarts and an impress-your-friends lasagne.

SIDES & SALADS

Simple extras like flatbreads and Yorkshire puddings that can be prepped in advance to save time later, and make-ahead salads for the perfect lunch on the go.

DESSERTS & BAKES

These chapters reveal sweet treats that store beautifully, including freezable cakes, puddings, ice cream, crumbles and muffins that work for everyday luxuries or for entertaining.

Every single recipe includes clear, detailed instructions for preparing, cooking, storing, freezing, defrosting and reheating, so you'll know what to do every step of the way and nothing will go to waste.

Getting started with batch cooking

You don't need a huge freezer or endless storage containers to get going. Start small. Try making extra portions of a recipe you already enjoy and freezing what you won't eat today. Make a breakfast ahead for tomorrow. Prep some extra vegetables while cooking tonight's dinner. These little wins will help build your confidence and momentum.

Here are some simple strategies to ease you into the habit:

DOUBLE IT

Are you cooking anyway? Make double the quantity. Freeze the extra for another day.

PLAN A LITTLE

Take 10–15 minutes before the start of the week to look at your schedule. Which nights will be busiest? What can be prepped or cooked ahead to relieve the pressure?

USE YOUR OVEN EFFICIENTLY

If it's already on, fill it. Roast two trays instead of one, bake multiple dishes together or cook tomorrow's dinner while prepping tonight's.

COMPONENT COOKING

Try getting ahead with things you know you'll enjoy eating – batch roast vegetables ahead of the weekend, cook a pot of grains to accompany midweek suppers or prep a protein to use in different meals throughout the week.

Your freezer is a powerful tool

The freezer is central to batch cooking. With a bit of organization, it becomes a reliable source of homemade ready meals, shortcuts and mealtime support.

Here are a few simple tips to get the most out of your freezer:

COOL BEFORE FREEZING

Always allow food to cool completely before freezing to prevent ice crystals and to maintain texture. Spread it out on a tray to speed up the cooling process if necessary.

PORTION WITH PURPOSE

Freeze in the portion sizes you'll actually use, whether that's single servings, couple-sized ones or family batches. Ice cube trays or reusable freezerproof containers make this really easy.

LABEL EVERYTHING

A strip of masking tape or individual freezer labels and a permanent marker are essential. Include the name of the dish you're freezing, the date of cooking and any reheating instructions.

USE SPACE-SAVING STORAGE

Stackable freezerproof containers are a convenient way of making the most of the room in your freezer. You can open-freeze some items, then wrap them individually and stack or slot into spaces in your freezer.

ALWAYS DEFROST SAFELY

Either defrost in the fridge overnight or at room temperature as directed, or reheat straight from frozen if appropriate.

KNOW YOUR SHELF LIFE

Cooked meat dishes	Up to three months
Soups and sauces	Up to three months
Marinated uncooked meat	Up to six months
Baked goods	Up to three months
Cooked grains and pasta	Up to one month

Make it work for you

It's easy to imagine batch cooking as a military-style operation with labelled tubs and rigid meal plans. In reality, it's far more flexible. Batch cooking is not about perfection. It's not about prepping 30 meals at once or filling the freezer in one day. It's not all-or-nothing. It's about making choices that help your future self: freezing a few spare portions of pasta sauce, prepping tomorrow's breakfast or planning ahead for a busy few days. It's about reducing stress and increasing satisfaction around food.

There's no one way to batch cook. For some, it's a Sunday afternoon routine. For others, it's about building a freezer stash gradually over time. Some might prefer complete ready-to-eat meals. Others may prefer to prep some ingredients and just freeze a meal base, in order to save time down the line. This book is designed to support all these approaches. Whether you're new to cooking or experienced in the kitchen, the goal is the same: to help you eat well with less daily effort.

With clear guidance, reliable recipes and plenty of storage tips, the chapters ahead will help you stock your fridge and freezer with food that's tasty, nourishing and ready when you are. Remember that whatever portion size is indicated in a recipe here, you can easily scale this up or down depending on your needs. Whether you're feeding a family, living solo, sharing a flat or just trying to make your week easier, batch cooking *can* work for you.

Let's get started! It's time to fill your kitchen with food that makes busy lives feel just that bit more manageable.

Breakfasts

✱ V

Prep: 15 mins
Cook: 20 mins

American Blueberry Pancakes

Makes 20 pancakes

400g (14oz) self-raising flour
2 tsp baking powder
2 eggs
600ml (20fl oz) milk
large knob of butter, melted
300g (10½oz) blueberries
2 tsp sunflower oil or a knob of butter, for cooking
golden syrup or maple syrup, to serve

1 Mix together the flour, baking powder and a pinch of salt in a large bowl. Beat the eggs with the milk in a jug. Make a well in the centre of the dry ingredients and whisk in the milk and egg mixture to make a thick smooth batter. Beat in the melted butter, then gently stir in half the blueberries. Any batter you want to keep for another day can now be frozen in a large ice cube tray. Once frozen, pop the ice cubes out into a freezerproof container and freeze for up to two months.

2 Heat the sunflower oil or butter in a large nonstick frying pan. Drop a large tablespoonful of the batter (or a couple of frozen ice cubes of batter) into the pan to make one fluffy pancake about 7.5cm (3 inches) across. Make three or four pancakes at a time.

3 Cook for about 3 mins over a medium heat until small bubbles appear on the surface of each pancake, then turn and cook for another 2–3 mins until golden. Remove to a plate and cover with kitchen paper to keep warm while you use up the rest of the batter. Serve with golden or maple syrup and the rest of the blueberries.

4 Any leftover cooked pancakes can be stored in the fridge for up to two days in an airtight container. You can also freeze cooked pancakes – store them, with baking parchment between each one, in an airtight container in the freezer for up to two months. Reheat chilled or frozen pancakes in 20-second blasts in the microwave.

NUTRITIONAL INFO

PER SERVING (WITHOUT SYRUP) KCAL **109** | FAT **2G** | SATURATES **1G** | CARBS **18G** | SUGARS **3G** | FIBRE **1G** | PROTEIN **4G** | SALT **0.41G**

✻ V

Prep: 10 mins
Cook: 20 mins, plus resting

Chocolate Crumpets

Makes 8–10

300ml (10fl oz) milk
200g (7oz) plain flour
2 tbsp cocoa powder
1 tsp fast-action dried yeast
2 tbsp golden caster sugar
2 tbsp vegetable oil, plus extra for the crumpet rings

To serve (optional)
dulce de leche or butter
flaky sea salt

1 Heat the milk in a pan until it just starts to bubble around the edges. Leave it to cool until it is tepid.

2 Remove 3 tbsp of the flour and put this back in the bag, then place the rest in a large mixing bowl with the cocoa powder, yeast and sugar. Stir in 250ml (9fl oz) of the milk, a little at a time, until you have a smooth batter. Cover and leave to rise in a warm place for 1 hr–1 hr 30 mins or until doubled in size and very bubbly. Stir in a little more of the milk if the batter is very thick – if it's too thick, the bubbles won't rise to the surface as well.

3 When risen, add the remaining milk to the batter to let it down a little. Lightly oil the insides of four 9cm (3½ inch) metal crumpet rings. Heat a large nonstick frying pan or griddle pan over a low–medium heat, add 1 tbsp of the oil and put the rings in the pan. Spoon the batter into the rings until they are half full. Let the crumpets cook slowly for about 10 mins or until the mixture has set and the bubbles on top have all popped. Lift the rings away carefully. Heat the remaining oil and repeat with the remaining mixture – you should get 8–10 crumpets in total. The cooked crumpets keep well, covered, in the fridge for up to 24 hrs, or can be kept in the freezer for up to one month and grilled from frozen.

4 Heat the grill to high. Transfer the pan (if it has a heatproof handle) to the grill and cook until the tops are golden brown. If the pan doesn't have a heatproof handle, or you're just getting your crumpets out of the fridge or freezer, transfer the crumpets to a baking sheet and grill them on that instead until hot and golden brown on top. Serve with your favourite crumpet toppings – we like dulce de leche or butter and flaky sea salt.

NUTRITIONAL INFO

PER CRUMPET (IF MAKING 10) KCAL **139** | FAT **4G** | SATURATES **1G** | CARBS **21G** | SUGARS **6G** | FIBRE **1G** | PROTEIN **4G** | SALT **0.03G**

✱ V Ve

Prep: 25 mins
Cook: 25 mins

Vegan Breakfast Muffins

Makes 12

150g (5½oz) muesli mix
50g (1¾oz) light brown soft sugar
160g (5¾oz) plain flour
1 tsp baking powder
250ml (9fl oz) sweetened soya milk
1 apple, peeled and grated
2 tbsp grapeseed oil
3 tbsp nut butter (we used almond)
4 tbsp demerara sugar
50g (1¾oz) pecans, roughly chopped

1 Heat the oven to 200°C/180°C fan/400°F/Gas Mark 6. Line a muffin tin with paper cases. Mix 100g (3½oz) of the muesli with the light brown sugar, flour and baking powder in a bowl.

2 Combine the milk, apple, oil and 2 tbsp of the nut butter in a jug, then stir into the dry mixture. Divide equally between the cases.

3 Mix the remaining muesli with the remaining nut butter, demerara sugar and the pecans, then spoon over the muffins.

4 Bake for 25–30 mins or until the muffins are risen and golden. These will keep for two to three days in an airtight container or in the freezer for one month. They can be refreshed in the microwave in 10–20-second blasts or in a low oven (120°C/100°C fan/250°F/Gas Mark ½) for 5 mins for a quick morning snack.

NUTRITIONAL INFO

PER SERVING KCAL **224** | FAT **9G** | SATURATES **1G** | CARBS **30G** | SUGARS **15G** | FIBRE **2G** | PROTEIN **4G** | SALT **0.1G**

✳

Prep: 30 mins
Cook: 30 mins

Sausage & Egg Muffins

Serves 12

500g (1lb 2 oz) minced beef
500g (1lb 2 oz) minced pork
1 tsp garlic powder
2 tsp dried mixed herbs
12 eggs
1 tsp vegetable oil
ketchup (optional)
12 English muffins, halved and toasted
12 slices of burger cheese

1. Heat the oven to 180° C/160° C fan/350° F/Gas Mark 4. Mix together the minced beef and minced pork, garlic powder, dried herbs and 1 tsp each of salt and black pepper in a large bowl. Form the sausage mixture into 12 evenly sized meatballs. Set aside.
2. Beat the eggs in a large jug with ½ tsp each of salt and black pepper. Pour into a baking tray, about 20 x 30cm (8 x 12 inches), lined with baking parchment, and bake for 15–20 mins until the egg is cooked through. Cut into 12 squares.
3. While the egg is cooking, heat the oil in a large frying pan. Put three or four of the meatballs in the frying pan and press down using a potato masher or large spoon to flatten. After 2–3 mins, flip them over and repeat, frying until they're cooked through – this should take about 6 mins in total.
4. Assemble your muffins by squirting a little ketchup, if using, on each toasted muffin base, then top with a cheese slice, an egg square, a sausage patty and more ketchup, if you like. Pop the top on each muffin. Wrap well in baking parchment and freeze in an airtight container for up to one month.
5. To reheat your muffins, defrost them in the fridge overnight, remove the baking parchment and microwave on full power for 30 seconds, then turn them over and microwave for a further 30 seconds. Check how warm they are in the middle, then repeat in 10–20 second blasts until hot. Alternatively, reheat in the oven at 180° C/160° C fan/350° F/ Gas Mark 4 for about 10 mins.

NUTRITIONAL INFO

PER SERVING KCAL **437** | FAT **22G** | SATURATES **9G** | CARBS **26G** | SUGARS **3G** | FIBRE **2G** | PROTEIN **33G** | SALT **2.11G**

V

Cinnamon Rolls

Prep: 40 mins, plus chilling
Cook: 40 mins

Makes 12

500g (1lb 2 oz) strong white bread flour, plus extra for dusting
7g (¼oz) sachet fast-action dried yeast
1 tsp ground cinnamon
50g (1¾oz) golden caster sugar
200ml (7fl oz) milk, warmed
2 eggs
1 tsp salt
100g (3½oz) unsalted butter, softened, plus extra for the tin
2 tbsp golden syrup

For the filling

150g (5½oz) light brown soft sugar
2 tbsp ground cinnamon
125g (4½oz) unsalted butter, at room temperature

For the icing

50g (1¾oz) soft cheese
50g (1¾oz) icing sugar
¼ tsp vanilla extract

1 Tip the flour, yeast, cinnamon, caster sugar, warmed milk, eggs and salt into the bowl of a stand mixer. Use a paddle attachment to combine everything until it begins to come together into a dough, then tip out onto a floured work surface and knead for about 2 mins until smooth. Put it back in the bowl and gradually add the softened butter, 1–2 tsp at a time, while mixing on a medium setting. Alternatively, knead the butter in by hand until smooth. Flatten the dough to a square roughly 20 x 20cm (8 x 8 inches), then cover and chill in the fridge for 1 hr.

2 Meanwhile, butter and line the base and sides of a deep baking tin, roughly 20 x 30cm (8 x 12 inches). To make the filling, mix the sugar with the cinnamon and a large pinch of sea salt in a large bowl, then set aside 2 tbsp of the mix in a small bowl. Add the butter to the large bowl and beat in to form a thick paste.

3 Lay the dough on a floured work surface and roll out into a neat rectangle roughly 25 x 35cm (10 x 14 inches). Spread over the filling to cover completely. Fold the bottom third of the dough into the middle, then fold over again to cover the top third. Chill the dough for another 30 mins.

4 Re-roll the dough into a rectangle about 30 x 40cm (12 x 16 inches), then roll it up along the long edge into a tight log. To get the neatest spirals, cut in half, lift onto a tray and freeze for 15 mins to firm up, then cut into 12 equal-sized slices. Arrange the slices, spiral side-up, in the prepared tin. Leave to prove in the fridge for at least 1 hr or up to 24 hrs.

5 Heat the oven to 200°C/180°C fan/400°F/Gas Mark 6. Bake the buns for 20 mins, then scatter over the reserved cinnamon sugar and bake for 10–15 mins until deep brown. They can now be frozen for two months.

6 Meanwhile, mix the golden syrup with 2 tsp boiling water. As soon as the buns come out of the oven, brush them with the syrup glaze, then leave to cool a little. To make the icing, beat the soft cheese, icing sugar and vanilla extract together in a bowl, then gradually add 1–2 tbsp boiling water to create a thick but pourable consistency. Drizzle the icing over the buns. These will keep for up to three days in an airtight container.

NUTRITIONAL INFO

PER SERVING KCAL **415** | FAT **18G** | SATURATES **11G** | CARBS **55G** | SUGARS **24G** | FIBRE **2G** | PROTEIN **8G** | SALT **0.9G**

V

Overnight Oats

Prep: 10 mins, plus chilling

Serves 2

½ tsp ground cinnamon
200ml (7fl oz) water or milk, plus a little more if needed
100g (3½oz) porridge oats
4 tbsp natural yogurt
100g (3½oz) mixed berries
drizzle of honey
1 tbsp nut butter (we used almond)

1 The night before serving, stir the cinnamon and the water or milk into the oats in a bowl with a pinch of salt. Divide between two containers or screw-top jars. Seal and leave overnight in the fridge – each one can be left for up to three days.

2 When you want to eat your oats, take them out of the fridge and loosen them with a little more water or milk if needed. Top with the yogurt, berries, honey and nut butter.

NUTRITIONAL INFO

PER SERVING KCAL **348** | FAT **11G** | SATURATES **2G** | CARBS **46.07G** | SUGARS **13G** | FIBRE **6G** | PROTEIN **13G** | SALT **0.17G**

V

Prep: 10 mins, plus chilling

Apple & Clementine Bircher Muesli

Serves 4

200g (7oz) porridge oats
½ tsp ground cinnamon
500ml (18fl oz) apple juice
4 apples, grated (we like Braeburn)
2 clementines, segmented
1 tbsp flaked almonds, toasted
2 tbsp pomegranate seeds

1. The night before, mix the oats with the cinnamon in a large bowl. Stir in the apple juice and grated apple, divide between four bowls or containers and cover. Leave overnight in the fridge. This will keep for up to two days.
2. When you're ready to eat, stir through the clementine segments, then scatter over the almonds and pomegranate seeds.

NUTRITIONAL INFO

PER SERVING KCAL **336** | FAT **6G** | SATURATES **1G** | CARBS **56G** | SUGARS **27G** | FIBRE **8G** | PROTEIN **11G** | SALT **0G**

V Ve

Nuts & Seeds Granola

Prep: 5 mins
Cook: 30 mins

Serves 10

150g (5½oz) rolled oats

150g (5½oz) mixed nuts (we used whole hazelnuts, flaked almonds and whole pecans)

50g (1¾oz) mixed seeds (we used a mixed bag containing sunflower, pumpkin, hemp and golden flaxseed)

50g (1¾oz) raisins

1 tsp ground cinnamon

¼ tsp sea salt

1 tsp almond extract (vanilla works well too, if you prefer)

50ml (2fl oz) vegetable oil

100ml (3½fl oz) maple syrup

To serve

milk or yogurt (or dairy-free alternative)

fruit (optional)

1 Heat the oven to 180°C/160°C fan/350°F/Gas Mark 4. Line a large baking tray with baking parchment. Put all the dry ingredients in a large mixing bowl. Whisk together the almond extract, vegetable oil and maple syrup in a jug, then pour into the bowl with the dry ingredients.

2 Mix together well, making sure that all the dry ingredients are well coated and that there are no dry bits. Tip the mixture onto the lined baking tray and spread out in an even layer. Bake for 25–30 mins until golden. You will need to give the mixture a few stirs every 8–10 mins to make sure it dries out evenly and doesn't clump together too much. Keep an eye on it, as nuts can burn easily.

3 Remove from the oven and leave to cool completely on the tray. Break up any large clumps of granola with a wooden spoon. Tip into an airtight container – it will keep for up to one month. Serve with milk or yogurt, and fresh seasonal fruit, if you like.

NUTRITIONAL INFO

PER SERVING KCAL **277** | FAT **18G** | SATURATES **2G** | CARBS **21G** | SUGARS **10G** | FIBRE **3G** | PROTEIN **6G** | SALT **0.1G**

Snacks & Sharers

✱

Prep: 20 mins
Cook: 40 mins

Ploughman's Sausage Rolls

Makes 10

- 8 caramelized onion sausages
- 5 pickled onions, finely chopped
- 50g (1¾oz) stilton, crumbled
- 3 tbsp pickle (preferably with small chunks)
- 100g (3½oz) extra-mature cheddar, grated
- plain flour, for dusting
- 500g (1lb 2oz) block of puff pastry
- 1 egg, beaten
- ½ tsp celery salt
- English mustard, to serve

1 Heat the oven to 200°C/180°C fan/400°F/Gas Mark 6. Line a baking tray with baking parchment. Squeeze the sausagemeat from the skins into a bowl. Tip in the pickled onions, stilton, pickle and most of the cheddar, reserving a small handful, and mix the ingredients together until well combined.

2 Lightly flour a clean work surface and roll out the pastry into a 30 x 40cm (12 x 16 inch) rectangle. Pat the sausagemeat into a long log shape that sits in the middle and down the length of the pastry rectangle. It should be about 5cm (2 inches) thick. Brush one of the long sides of pastry with some beaten egg, then fold the other side over to encase the sausagement. Fold the egg-washed side over the top and press gently to seal. Trim the excess pastry, making sure the overlap is about 3cm (1¼ inches). Carefully turn over the sausage roll so that the seal is at the bottom. Using a sharp knife, carefully cut into pieces 4cm (1½ inches) wide and arrange on the lined baking tray – you should get 10 sausage roll slices.

3 You can now freeze some of the sausage rolls for another day. Open-freeze them on a tray until solid, then transfer to a freezerproof container and freeze for up to three months. Defrost in the fridge overnight, then cook as below, adding an extra 5 mins.

4 To cook the sausage rolls, brush them with the remaining beaten egg, then scatter over the remaining cheddar and the celery salt. Bake for 35–40 mins until golden and cooked through. Leave to cool on the tray for 10–15 mins before serving warm with English mustard for dunking.

NUTRITIONAL INFO

PER SERVING KCAL **398** | FAT **28G** | SATURATES **13G** | CARBS **22G** | SUGARS **5G** | FIBRE **2G** | PROTEIN **14G** | SALT **1.7G**

✳

Prep: 30 mins, plus rising
Cook: 30 mins

Chorizo, Rocket & Preserved Lemon Calzones

Makes 4

500g (1lb 2 oz) strong white bread flour, plus extra for dusting
2 tbsp paprika
1½ tsp fast-action dried yeast
1 tbsp olive oil, plus extra for the bowl
semolina, for dusting

For the filling

100g (3½oz) cooking chorizo, sliced
2 garlic cloves, crushed
350ml (12fl oz) passata
1 tbsp light brown soft sugar
1 tbsp red wine vinegar
2 small preserved lemons, quartered, pith removed and zest finely chopped
½ small bunch of basil, roughly chopped
50g (1¾oz) rocket, roughly chopped
75g (2¾oz) mozzarella, torn into chunks
25g (1oz) parmesan, grated

1 For the dough, put the flour, paprika, yeast, oil, 300ml (10fl oz) lukewarm water and a large pinch of salt in a bowl. Mix into a soft, slightly wet dough. Knead in a stand mixer fitted with a dough hook or by hand for 10 mins until smooth (it will still be quite soft). Tip into an oiled bowl, cover and leave to rise for 2 hrs.

2 Meanwhile, make the filling. Fry the chorizo in a large saucepan over a medium heat for 2 mins until some of its oils have been released. Add the garlic and continue to fry for 30 seconds. Add the passata, sugar, vinegar and preserved lemons and simmer for 5 mins until thick. Stir in the basil and rocket. Leave to cool.

3 Heat the oven to 200°C/180°C fan/400°F/Gas Mark 6 with a baking tray inside. Divide the dough into four pieces, then roll each out on a lightly floured work surface into a thin 30cm (12 inch) circle. Lay each circle on a square of baking parchment dusted with semolina. Spread the cooled filling over half of each circle, leaving a border, then top with some of the mozzarella. Brush around the edge of each circle with a little water. Working with one circle at a time, fold one half over the other so that the filling is enclosed, then crimp the edge to seal. The calzones can now be frozen for up to three months, wrapped in baking parchment, then a layer of foil.

4 Lift the calzones on the parchment squares onto the hot baking tray in the oven, sprinkle the parmesan on top and bake for 15–20 mins until puffed up and golden brown. To bake from frozen, remove the foil, then lay the calzones flat on their baking parchment wrapping on the hot baking sheet in the hot oven. Bake for 35–45 mins until golden.

NUTRITIONAL INFO

PER CALZONE KCAL **742** | FAT **19G** | SATURATES **8G** | CARBS **108G** | SUGARS **10G** | FIBRE **7G** | PROTEIN **31G** | SALT **1.5G**

Ham Croquetas

Prep: 25 mins, plus chilling
Cook: 35 mins

Makes 15–20

75g (2¾oz) plain flour
2 large eggs, beaten
75g (2¾oz) dried breadcrumbs
1.4 litres (2½ pints) sunflower oil, for frying

For the filling

4 tbsp extra virgin olive oil, plus extra for your hands
½ small leek, very finely chopped
70g (2½oz) jamón Ibérico or other air-dried ham, very finely chopped
60g (2¼oz) plain flour
75ml (2½fl oz) ham or vegetable stock
325ml (11fl oz) whole milk
freshly grated nutmeg

1 To make the filling, heat the olive oil in a pan, then add the leek and sauté until soft but not coloured. Stir in the ham and fry for 1 min, then stir in the flour and fry over a medium heat, stirring occasionally, until the mixture is golden but not burnt – this will take about 5 mins.

2 Meanwhile, combine the stock and milk in a small pan and heat until steaming but not boiling. Season with a few scrapes of nutmeg. Gradually add the liquid to the ham and leeks, stirring constantly. Once you've incorporated all the liquid, continue to cook the filling over a medium heat for about 10 mins or until it thickens – it has to be really thick because you don't want the croquetas to turn into pancakes. Season with black pepper, then taste and add a little salt if necessary – the ham can be very salty to start with. Smooth the mixture onto a baking tray, 20 x 30cm (8 x 12 inches). Once it has stopped steaming, cover the tray to stop the mixture drying out. Leave to cool before chilling in the fridge for 1 hr.

3 To make the croquetas, line up three bowls – the first filled with the flour, the second with the beaten eggs and the third with the breadcrumbs. Take the ham mixture out of the fridge. Put a little olive oil on your hands, then roll a walnut-sized spoonful of the mixture between your palms. You should be able to make 15–20 croquetas out of the mixture. Dunk each one into the flour – you want a dusting – followed by the egg, then the breadcrumbs. Put them on a tray and chill in the fridge for 30 mins. You can now open-freeze the croquetas until solid, then transfer them to a freezerproof container and freeze for one month.

4 If you have a deep-fat fryer, heat the oil to 180°C/350°F and fry for 2 mins. Alternatively, heat the oil in a deep, heavy-based saucepan until it starts to shimmer. Then add five or six croquetas at a time and fry until golden all over and hot right through to the middle. Remove, drain on kitchen paper and eat straight away. If cooking from frozen, cook the croquetas on a baking tray lined with baking parchment in the oven at 200°C/180°C fan/400°F/Gas Mark 6 for 8 mins.

NUTRITIONAL INFO

PER CROQUETA (IF MAKING 20) KCAL **99** | FAT **6G** | SATURATES **1G** | CARBS **9G** | SUGARS **1G** | FIBRE **0G** | PROTEIN **3G** | SALT **0.3G**

✳ V

Prep: 25 mins
Cook: 45 mins

Jamaican Veggie Patties

Makes 16–20

1 tbsp vegetable oil
1 onion, finely chopped
3 large garlic cloves, crushed
3 tsp mild curry powder
3 tbsp finely sliced chives
2 tbsp chopped thyme leaves
250g (9oz) mixed vegetables (a mixture of sweetcorn, carrots, peas and peppers is great), finely chopped where required
100ml (3½fl oz) vegetable stock
1 tsp light brown soft sugar
1–2 tsp hot pepper sauce (optional)
1 slice of any bread of your choice (about 60g/ 2¼oz), torn into small pieces
500g (1lb 2oz) block of shortcrust pastry
plain flour, for dusting
1 tsp turmeric
1 egg, beaten
your favourite hot sauce, to serve

1 Heat the oil in a deep, lidded saucepan over a medium heat and cook the onion with a small pinch of salt for 8–10 mins, stirring regularly, until softened. Add the garlic, 2 tsp of the curry powder and the herbs and stir for about 30 seconds until fragrant.

2 Add the mixed vegetables, stock, sugar and hot pepper sauce, if using. Turn the heat up to high and bring the mixture to the boil, then reduce the heat to low, cover and simmer for about 10 mins. Add the bread, then continue to simmer over a low heat for another 8–10 mins, stirring occasionally, until thickened. Taste for seasoning and leave to cool.

3 Roll the pastry out on a lightly floured work surface to a 5mm (¼ inch) thickness. Stamp out 16–20 circles (about 8cm/3¼ inch in diameter) using a biscuit cutter, then spoon the cooled filling over one half of each pastry circle. Fold the other half of the pastry over to enclose the filling and create a semi-circle, then crimp the edge with a fork to seal.

4 You can now freeze some of the patties for another day. Put the patties on a baking tray lined with baking parchment and open-freeze until solid. Transfer to a freezerproof container, seal and freeze for up to two months. Defrost in the fridge overnight before cooking as below, or bake the patties from frozen, simply adding an extra 5 mins to the cooking time.

5 Heat the oven to 220°C/200°C fan/425°F/Gas Mark 7. Arrange the patties on a baking tray lined with baking parchment. Whisk the turmeric and remaining tsp curry powder into the beaten egg, then brush this over the patties. Bake for 18–20 mins (or 25 mins from frozen) until the pastry is golden and cooked through, then serve immediately with your favourite hot sauce.

NUTRITIONAL INFO

PER SERVING KCAL **144** | FAT **9G** | SATURATES **3G** | CARBS **13G** | SUGARS **2G** | FIBRE **1G** | PROTEIN **3G** | SALT **0.22G**

✳ V

Prep: 30 mins, plus rising
Cook: 15 mins

Bake-From-the-Freezer Pizzas

Makes 6

- 500g (1lb 2oz) pack of bread mix or pizza base mix
- neutral oil, for the bowl and trays
- plain flour, for dusting
- 6 tbsp tomato pasta sauce or passata
- 250g (9oz) ball mozzarella
- small bunch of basil leaves, shredded
- 18 cherry tomatoes, halved
- 25g (1oz) parmesan (or vegetarian alternative), grated

1 Make up the bread dough following pack instructions. Transfer to an oiled bowl to rise for about 1 hr.

2 Knock back in the bowl by squashing all the air out of the dough with your fist. Divide the dough into six and roll each one on a lightly floured work surface to a circle about 18cm (7 inches) in diameter. Put any dough you're not using under a damp tea towel to stop it drying out.

3 Put the pizza bases on large, oiled baking trays – you may need two or three. Spread 1 tbsp sauce or passata on each base. Tear the mozzarella ball into pieces, patting them dry with kitchen paper to keep the base crispy. Scatter the basil, tomatoes, mozzarella and parmesan over the bases (you can add whatever you fancy).

4 You can freeze the pizzas now, if you like, on the baking trays, wrapped, for up to two months. You can also open-freeze the pizzas until solid, then lift them off the trays and stack, using sheets of baking parchment in between each one. Then wrap the whole stack or put in a large freezerproof container – perfect if you'll be grabbing just one or two at a time.

5 If eating straight away, heat the oven to 240°C/220°C fan/475°F/Gas Mark 9. Bake for 8–12 mins until crisp and golden. To cook from frozen, remove any wrapping and put on large, oiled baking trays if not already on them. Heat the oven to 220°C/200°C fan/425°F/Gas Mark 7. Bake for 10–14 mins until crisp and golden.

NUTRITIONAL INFO

PER SERVING KCAL **380** | FAT **13G** | SATURATES **7G** | CARBS **51G** | SUGARS **4G** | FIBRE **5G** | PROTEIN **18G** | SALT **2.53G**

✳ V

Prep: 25 mins
Cook: 45 mins

Cheese & Spinach Pie

Serves 9–12

vegetable oil, for the tin
4 eggs
500g (1lb 2oz) curd cheese, crumbled (this can be found in specialist shops), or 250g (9oz) ricotta mixed with 250g (9oz) mascarpone
250g (9oz) feta, crumbled
2 tbsp soured cream or crème fraîche
500g (1lb 2oz) frozen spinach, defrosted and excess moisture wrung out in a clean tea towel
100ml (3½fl oz) olive oil
300ml (10fl oz) natural yogurt
1 tsp baking powder
500g (1lb 2oz) filo pastry sheets
20g (¾oz) unsalted butter

1. Lightly oil a roasting tin measuring about 25 x 35cm (10 x 14 inches) and 4cm (1½ inches) deep, then line with baking parchment. Mix the eggs, cheeses, soured cream or crème fraîche, spinach and some seasoning together in a bowl. In another bowl, mix together the olive oil, yogurt and baking powder.
2. Cut the filo sheets in half so that they are roughly the size of the tin. Put one filo sheet in the tin and evenly brush over 1–2 tbsp of the yogurt mixture using a pastry brush. Top with another filo sheet, brush over more yogurt mixture and repeat until you've used half the filo sheets and roughly half the yogurt mixture.
3. Pour over the cheese filling, then gently spread it to the edges using a spatula. Continue layering the rest of the filo sheets and yogurt mixture. Spread any remaining yogurt mixture over the top of the final filo sheet.
4. Cut the pie into squares (either nine or twelve, depending on how big you want the pieces to be). You can now freeze the squares for up to a month. Defrost completely in the fridge overnight before cooking.
5. To cook, heat the oven to 200°C/180°C fan/400°F/Gas Mark 6. Top each square with a small knob of the butter, then bake for 20 mins. Reduce the oven to 180°C/160°C fan/350°F/Gas Mark 4 and bake for another 25–30 mins until browned on top. Leave to cool slightly before serving warm. You can cover the squares and keep them in the fridge for up to two days.

NUTRITIONAL INFO

PER SERVING (IF SERVING 12) KCAL **445** | FAT **30G** | SATURATES **14G** | CARBS **27G** | SUGARS **5G** | FIBRE **3G** | PROTEIN **15G** | SALT **1.2G**

✱ V

Prep: 20 mins
Cook: 1 hr and 5 mins

Roasted Tomato, Sweetcorn, Thyme & Feta Cornbread

Serves 8–10

- 300g (10½oz) tomatoes (a mixture of sizes and colours is nice), small ones left whole, larger ones halved or quartered
- 1 large sweetcorn cob
- 2 tbsp olive oil
- 225g (8oz) fine cornmeal
- 140g (5oz) plain flour
- 1 tbsp golden caster sugar
- 2 tsp baking powder
- 500ml (18fl oz) full-fat natural yogurt
- 3 eggs
- 75g (2¾oz) butter, melted
- 200g (7oz) feta, crumbled
- 6 thyme sprigs, leaves picked

1 Heat the oven to 220°C/200°C fan/425°F/Gas Mark 7. Put the tomatoes and sweetcorn cob in a roasting tin, drizzle with half the oil, season with salt and roast for 12 mins. When cooked, you can keep the tomatoes and sweetcorn cob in the fridge for up to one day. Just before using, cut the kernels off the cob.

2 Reduce the oven to 200°C/180°C fan/400°F/Gas Mark 6. Line a 23cm (9 inch) cake tin or ovenproof frying pan with a large sheet of baking parchment. Tip the cornmeal, flour, sugar, baking powder and ½ tsp salt into a large bowl. Beat the yogurt, eggs and melted butter together in a small bowl using a fork. Pour the wet ingredients into the dry, then add most of the sweetcorn, feta and thyme (reserving a handful of each for the top). Mix together with a spatula until just combined.

3 Pour the batter into the lined tin or pan. Sprinkle over the reserved sweetcorn and feta, then arrange the tomatoes on top along with the rest of the thyme. Drizzle with the remaining oil, then bake for 50 mins until golden and a skewer inserted into the middle comes out clean, with no wet batter clinging to it.

4 Leave to cool in the tin for 10 mins, then cut into wedges and serve warm. Once completely cool, the cornbread will keep in an airtight container for up to two days or frozen for up to a month.

NUTRITIONAL INFO

PER SERVING (IF SERVING 10) KCAL **342** | FAT **17G** | SATURATES **25G** | CARBS **10G** | SUGARS **7G** | FIBRE **3G** | PROTEIN **20G** | SALT **0.1G**

✻ V Ve

Vegetable Gyoza

Prep: 2 hrs, plus chilling
Cook: 20 mins

Makes 25

250g (9oz) plain flour
1 tsp salt
cornflour, for dusting

For the filling
200g (7oz) white cabbage
4 chestnut mushrooms
1 carrot
4 water chestnuts (optional)
thumb-sized piece of ginger, peeled and finely grated
2 garlic cloves, finely grated
3 spring onions, finely sliced
2 tbsp sunflower oil, plus extra for frying the gyoza
1 tbsp soy sauce
1 tbsp saké, Shaohsing rice wine or dry sherry

For the dipping sauce
6 tbsp soy sauce
2 tbsp rice wine vinegar
crispy chilli oil (optional)

TIP

Alternatively, you can use 25–30 shop-bought gyoza skins.

1 To make the gyoza dough, tip the flour and salt into a bowl. Bring a kettle to the boil and measure out 150ml (5fl oz) boiling water. Slowly pour the water over the flour while mixing with a spoon to form a stiff dough. When the dough is cool enough to handle, tip onto a work surface and knead for 10 mins until smooth. Wrap the dough and chill for at least 1 hr.

2 Meanwhile, coarsely grate the cabbage, mushrooms, carrot and water chestnuts, if using, then tip into a bowl. Add the ginger, garlic and spring onions. Heat the oil in a wok, then tip in all the veg and stir-fry over a high heat for 3 mins until softened. Drizzle over the soy sauce and saké, rice wine or sherry and cook for 2–3 mins. Season to taste. Tip back into the bowl to cool completely.

3 Divide the dough in two. Scatter a work surface generously with cornflour and roll one ball of dough out until paper-thin. Use a 10cm (4 inch) cutter to cut out circles of dough and pile them up (they won't stick because of the cornflour). Repeat with all the dough, re-rolling the trimmings, until you have about 25 skins.

4 To assemble, sprinkle more cornflour on a tray and have a bowl of cold water ready. Hold a skin in the palm of one hand and put a teaspoon of filling in the centre. Dip your finger in the water and wipe around the inside edge of the skin. Bring the edges of the skin together, pinching pleats along one side. To freeze, space them out on a baking tray and open-freeze, then tip into a freezerproof container and return to the freezer for up to three months.

5 To cook the gyoza, take them out of the freezer, if frozen, and heat a drizzle of oil in a nonstick frying pan with a lid. Fry the gyoza for 2 mins, flat-side down, until golden. Add 100ml (3½fl oz) water to the pan and cover. Cook over a medium heat for 3–5 mins until the water has evaporated and the gyoza are cooked through. Remove the lid and leave the gyoza to sizzle on the bottom for a minute. Mix the dipping sauce ingredients together, then serve with the gyoza.

NUTRITIONAL INFO

PER SERVING KCAL **62** | FAT **2G** | SATURATES **0G** | CARBS **10G** | SUGARS **2G** | FIBRE **1G** | PROTEIN **1G** | SALT **0.7G**

✱ V

Prep: 25 mins
Cook: 20 mins

Brie & Cranberry Filo Parcels

Makes 18

6 filo pastry sheets
75g (2¾oz) butter, melted
4 tbsp cranberry sauce, plus extra to serve
100g (3½oz) brie (or vegetarian alternative), cut into 18 pieces
1 tbsp poppy seeds

1 Heat the oven to 200°C/180°C fan/400°F/Gas Mark 6 and line two baking trays with baking parchment. Unravel a sheet of filo pastry onto a chopping board, covering the rest of the filo with a damp tea towel so that it doesn't dry out. Brush the filo sheet liberally with some of the melted butter, then cut into three strips lengthways.

2 Spoon ½ tsp cranberry sauce over the top right-hand corner of each pastry strip and place a piece of brie on top. Fold the pastry over the filling to create a triangle, then continue to fold the pastry over itself down the length of the strip. Brush with more butter to seal, then sprinkle over a few of the poppy seeds and place on a lined baking tray. Repeat with the remaining ingredients. The parcels can be covered and chilled in the fridge for up to one day or frozen for up to three months.

3 Bake for 15–20 mins (or 20–25 mins from frozen) until deep golden brown. Leave to stand for 5 mins before serving with some extra cranberry sauce.

NUTRITIONAL INFO

PER SERVING KCAL **78** | FAT **6G** | SATURATES **3G** | CARBS **5G** | SUGARS **1G** | FIBRE **0.2G** | PROTEIN **2G** | SALT **0.2G**

Soups

Wonton Soup

Prep: 20 mins
Cook: 10 mins

Serves 4 plus leftovers

200g (7oz) pack of frozen wonton wrappers, defrosted
plain flour, for dusting

For the wonton filling

2 garlic cloves, grated
1 tbsp grated ginger
300g (10½oz) minced pork
150g (5½oz) raw prawns, peeled, de-veined and roughly chopped into 5mm (¼ inch) pieces
1 spring onion, finely chopped
1 tbsp Shaohsing rice wine
1 tbsp light soy sauce
1 tsp toasted sesame oil
pinch of white pepper
1 tsp cornflour

For the soup broth

2 tsp vegetable bouillon powder
2 tbsp grated ginger
2 tbsp light soy sauce
2 tsp toasted sesame oil
400g (14oz) baby pak choi, leaves separated
400g (14oz) cooked egg noodles (optional)

To serve

4 spring onions, finely sliced
chilli oil (optional)

1 For the wonton filling, mix together the garlic, ginger, minced pork, prawns, spring onion and some seasoning in a bowl. Add the remaining filling ingredients and mix well again.

2 Take around 15g (½oz) of the filling and place in the centre of a wonton wrapper. Bring all the sides to the centre, pinching and twisting the top to secure. Repeat with the rest of the wonton wrappers. Set half the dumplings aside on a lightly floured tray. The remaining wontons can be frozen – open-freeze them on a tray for 12 hrs, then transfer to a freezerproof container and freeze for up to three months.

3 You can cook the wontons fresh or from frozen. Put 1.4 litres (2½ pints) water in a pan, add the bouillon powder and bring to the boil. Add the ginger, soy sauce and sesame oil to the stock. Gently drop in the wontons and baby pak choi and reduce the heat to simmer until the wontons float to the surface – this will take 4–5 mins. If serving with noodles, drop in the cooked egg noodles for the final minute to warm through. Serve the wontons in the broth, with spring onions sprinkled over and a drizzle of chilli oil, if you like.

NUTRITIONAL INFO

PER SERVING KCAL **248** | FAT **8G** | SATURATES **2G** | CARBS **23G** | SUGARS **3G** | FIBRE **3G** | PROTEIN **20G** | SALT **2.78G**

✳

Prep: 15 mins
Cook: 25 mins

Cavolo Nero, Meatball & Cannellini Soup

Serves 4

2 tbsp olive or rapeseed oil
6 sausages (we used Cumberland)
1 red onion, finely chopped
3 garlic cloves, crushed
½–1 tsp chilli flakes (optional)
200g (7oz) cavolo nero, kale or other hardy greens, chopped
2 x 400g (14oz) cans cannellini beans
1 chicken stock cube
zest of 1 lemon, plus juice of ½
crusty bread, to serve (optional)

1 Heat the oil in a large, lidded pan. Squeeze the sausagemeat from the skins into the pan in rough meatball shapes – you should get about five meatballs from each sausage. Fry the meatballs for 5–7 mins until browned all over, then scoop onto a plate. Add the onion to the pan and cook for about 8 mins until softened, then stir in the garlic and chilli flakes, if using, and cook for a further minute.

2 Add the remaining ingredients to the pan along with the meatballs and 700ml (1¼ pints) hot water. Season and stir, then cover and simmer for 8–10 mins until the greens have wilted and the meatballs are cooked through. Add a little more water if you want a soupier consistency. You can now freeze the soup. Leave to cool completely, then transfer to a freezerproof container and freeze for up to three months. Defrost in the fridge overnight, then reheat in a pan with a splash of water until the meatballs are piping hot throughout.

3 Serve in shallow bowls with crusty bread, if you like.

NUTRITIONAL INFO

PER SERVING KCAL **470** | FAT **27G** | SATURATES **8G** | CARBS **34G** | SUGARS **6G** | FIBRE **6G** | PROTEIN **19G** | SALT **2.3G**

Chicken Noodle Soup

Prep: 10 mins
Cook: 30 mins

Serves 4

- 1.8 litres (3¼ pints) chicken or vegetable stock or miso soup
- 2 skinless chicken breasts (about 175g/6oz each)
- 2 tsp finely chopped fresh ginger
- 2 garlic cloves, finely chopped
- 100g (3½oz) dried rice or wheat noodles
- 4 tbsp sweetcorn, canned or frozen
- 4–6 mushrooms, thinly sliced
- 4 spring onions, shredded
- 4 tsp soy sauce, plus extra for serving

To serve (optional)

- mint or basil leaves
- shredded red chilli

1. Pour the stock into a large, lidded pan and add the chicken breasts, ginger and garlic. Bring to the boil, then reduce the heat, partially cover and simmer for 20 mins until the chicken is tender.
2. Put the chicken on a chopping board and shred into bite-size pieces using a couple of forks. Return the chicken to the stock with the noodles, sweetcorn, mushrooms, most of the spring onion, and the soy sauce. Simmer for 3–4 mins until the noodles are tender. If you want to freeze some or all of the soup for another day, leave out the noodles and leave to cool completely, then transfer to a freezerproof container and freeze for up to three months. Cook the noodles separately following pack instructions when you're reheating the soup, then add just before serving.
3. Ladle into four bowls and scatter over the remaining spring onion, and the mint or basil leaves and chilli, if using. Serve with extra soy sauce.

NUTRITIONAL INFO

PER SERVING KCAL **266** | FAT **2G** | SATURATES **0.4G** | CARBS **26G** | SUGARS **3G** | FIBRE **3G** | PROTEIN **34G** | SALT **3.2G**

✳ V Ve

Prep: 10 mins
Cook: 40 mins

Spiced Lentil & Butternut Squash Soup

Serves 4–6

2 tbsp olive oil
2 onions, finely chopped
2 garlic cloves, crushed
¼ tsp hot chilli powder
1 tbsp ras el hanout
1 butternut squash, peeled, deseeded and cut into 2cm (¾ inch) pieces
100g (3½oz) dried red lentils
1 litre (1¾ pints) vegetable stock
small bunch of coriander, leaves chopped, plus extra to serve

To serve

dukkah
natural yogurt (or dairy-free alternative)

1. Heat the oil in a large, lidded flameproof casserole dish or saucepan over a medium–high heat. Fry the onions with a pinch of salt for 7 mins or until softened and just caramelized. Add the garlic, chilli and ras el hanout and cook for 1 min more.
2. Stir in the squash and lentils. Pour over the stock and season to taste. Bring to the boil, then reduce the heat to a simmer, cover and cook for 25 mins or until the squash is soft. Blitz the soup with a hand blender until smooth, then season to taste.
3. If you're not planning to eat all the soup immediately, leave to cool completely, then transfer to a freezerproof container. Defrost in the fridge overnight, then reheat until piping hot before serving.
4. Stir in the chopped coriander and ladle the soup into bowls. Serve topped with dukkah, yogurt and extra coriander.

NUTRITIONAL INFO

PER SERVING (IF SERVING 6) KCAL **167** | FAT **5G** | SATURATES **1G** | CARBS **23G** | SUGARS **4G** | FIBRE **3G** | PROTEIN **6G** | SALT **0.5G**

✳ V Ve

Prep: 10 mins
Cook: 25 mins

Red Lentil, Chickpea & Chilli Soup

Serves 4

2 tsp cumin seeds
large pinch of chilli flakes
1 tbsp olive oil
1 red onion, chopped
140g (5oz) dried red lentils
850ml (1½ pints) vegetable stock or water
400g (14oz) can tomatoes, whole or chopped
200g (7oz) can chickpeas or ½ a 400g (14oz) can, drained and rinsed (you can freeze leftovers)
small bunch of coriander, roughly chopped
4 tbsp 0% fat Greek yogurt (or dairy-free alternative), to serve

1. Heat a large saucepan and dry-fry the cumin seeds and chilli flakes for 1 min or until they start to jump around the pan and release their aromas. Add the oil and onion and cook for 5 mins.
2. Stir in the lentils, stock or water and the tomatoes, then bring to the boil. Simmer for 15 mins until the lentils have softened.
3. Whizz the soup with a hand blender or in a food processor until it is a rough purée. Pour back into the pan and add the chickpeas. You can now freeze the soup until required – either defrost in the fridge overnight or cook from frozen over a low heat with a generous splash of water until piping hot.
4. Heat gently, season well and stir in most of the chopped coriander, reserving a few leaves to serve. Finish the soup with the yogurt and remaining coriander.

NUTRITIONAL INFO

PER SERVING KCAL **259** | FAT **5G** | SATURATES **1G** | CARBS **33G** | SUGARS **10G** | FIBRE **7G** | PROTEIN **17G** | SALT **0.62G**

✻ V

Prep: 30 mins
Cook: 1 hr and 30 mins

Next-Level Tomato Soup

Serves 6

1.2kg (2lb 10oz) ripe tomatoes of your choice (we like plum), halved
6 garlic cloves, sliced
½ red chilli, sliced (optional)
30g (1oz) golden caster sugar, plus a little extra if needed
1 tsp dried oregano
100ml (3½fl oz) red wine vinegar
100ml (3½fl oz) olive oil
large bunch of basil
2 onions, sliced
400ml (14fl oz) vegetable stock

For the croutons (optional)

200g (7oz) white bread, sourdough or another whole loaf (preferably slightly stale), crusts trimmed away
2 tbsp olive oil
10g (¼oz) parmesan (or vegetarian alternative), finely grated (optional)

NUTRITIONAL INFO

PER SERVING KCAL **236** | FAT **17G** | SATURATES **2G** | CARBS **16G** | SUGARS **14G** | FIBRE **4G** | PROTEIN **3G** | SALT **0.2G**

1 Heat the oven to 200°C/180°C fan/400°F/Gas Mark 6. Line a large, shallow roasting tin with baking parchment and arrange the tomatoes in the tin, cut-side up. Season generously with salt, then scatter with the garlic, chilli, if using, 1 tsp of the sugar and the oregano. Drizzle with 1 tbsp of the vinegar and 1 tbsp of the oil. Roast for 45 mins until the tomatoes are shrivelled and have released plenty of juice.

2 If making the croutons, tear the bread into small pieces and tip onto a baking tray. Drizzle with the oil and scatter with the parmesan, if using. Toss to coat the bread in the oil and cheese. Bake alongside the tomatoes for 20–25 mins, tossing a few times until golden and crunchy. Remove from the oven and set aside to cool. The croutons will keep in an airtight container for one day.

3 Meanwhile, pick and set aside a large handful of basil leaves, reserving the stalks and remaining sprigs. Heat another 2 tbsp of the oil in a saucepan or frying pan over a medium–low heat and cook the onions with a little salt for 20 mins until soft and sticky. Stir in the rest of the sugar, then pour over the remaining vinegar. Bring to the boil, then simmer for 3–5 mins until the onions have broken down a little and the liquid is syrupy.

4 Tip the tomatoes, along with their roasting juices, into the pan with the onions, then pour in the stock and scatter over the basil stalks and whole sprigs. Stir well and bring to the boil, then reduce the heat and simmer for 20 mins until the tomatoes have broken down into a chunky sauce. Remove from the heat and leave to cool slightly, then tip everything into a food processor or blender and blitz until the soup is as smooth as you like. Alternatively, use a hand blender (you may need to blitz the soup in batches). For an even smoother soup, you can pass it through a sieve. Season the soup and add a little more sugar if needed. You can either serve your soup immediately, or cool completely and keep in the fridge in a non-metallic airtight container for up to three days or in the freezer for up to three months. Defrost in the fridge overnight before reheating and serving as below.

5 Crush the reserved basil leaves with a pinch of salt to a paste using a pestle and mortar. Stir this into the remaining oil to make a bright green basil oil. Tip the soup into a clean pan and reheat until piping hot, then ladle into bowls. Drizzle with the basil oil, then scatter with the cheesy, crunchy croutons, if using.

✳ V Ve

Prep: 15 mins
Cook: 35 mins

Sweet Potato & Carrot Soup

Serves 4

500g (1lb 2oz) sweet potatoes, peeled and cut into chunks

300g (10½oz) carrots, peeled and cut into chunks

3 tbsp olive oil

2 onions, finely chopped

2 garlic cloves, crushed

1 litre (1¾ pints) vegetable stock

100ml (3½fl oz) crème fraîche (or dairy-free alternative), plus extra to serve

1 Heat the oven to 220°C/200°C fan/425°F/Gas Mark 7 and put the sweet potatoes and carrots into a large roasting tin. Drizzle with 2 tbsp of the oil, add plenty of seasoning and mix well. Roast the vegetables for 25–30 mins or until caramelized and tender.

2 Meanwhile, put the remaining oil in a large, deep saucepan and fry the onions over a medium–low heat for about 10 mins until softened. Add the garlic and stir for 1 min before adding the stock. Simmer for 5–10 mins until the onions are very soft, then set aside.

3 Once the roasted vegetables are done, leave to cool a little, then transfer to the saucepan and use a hand blender to blitz until smooth. Stir in the crème fraîche and a little more seasoning and reheat until hot. If you're not planning to eat all the soup immediately, leave to cool completely, then transfer to a freezerproof container and freeze for up to three months. Defrost in the fridge overnight, then reheat until piping hot before serving.

4 Serve in bowls topped with a swirl of crème fraîche and a good grinding of black pepper.

NUTRITIONAL INFO

PER SERVING KCAL **419** | FAT **19G** | SATURATES **8G** | CARBS **45G** | SUGARS **27G** | FIBRE **10G** | PROTEIN **11G** | SALT **0.9G**

✱ V Ve

Prep: 35 mins
Cook: 1 hr

Spiced Pumpkin Soup

Serves 4

- 1 pumpkin, about 1.5–2kg (3lb 5oz–4lb 8oz)
- 1 tbsp garam masala, plus an extra pinch if you like
- 2 tsp ground coriander
- 2 tsp ground cumin
- 3 tbsp olive oil
- 1 onion, finely chopped
- thumb-sized piece of ginger, peeled and finely chopped
- 2 garlic cloves, finely chopped
- ½–1 tsp chilli flakes or powder, plus an extra pinch if you like
- 900ml (1⅔ pints) vegetable stock
- 100ml (3½fl oz) double cream or crème fraîche (or dairy-free alternative), plus extra to serve

TIP

You can toast the pumpkin seeds to sprinkle on top. Wash the seeds well and remove any strings and flesh. Dry and toss in oil and any spices you like. Transfer to a baking tray and toast in the oven for 10–15 mins until golden and crisp.

1. Heat the oven to 180°C/160°C fan/350°F/Gas Mark 4. Cut the pumpkin into wedges or chunks (keep the skin on) and tip into a bowl. Put the garam masala and 1 tsp each of the coriander and cumin into a small bowl and mix with 2 tbsp of the oil, then season. Drizzle over the pumpkin and toss well to coat in the spiced oil. Transfer to a baking tray, spread out evenly and roast for 40–45 mins, turning halfway through cooking, until the pumpkin is very soft when pierced with a fork. Leave to cool on the tray for a few minutes.
2. Heat the remaining oil in a large saucepan and fry the onion with a pinch of salt for 10 mins until soft. Add the ginger, garlic, remaining spices and chilli and fry for a few more minutes until fragrant. Pour in the stock and bring to a gentle simmer.
3. When the pumpkin is cool enough to touch, use a spoon to scoop the soft flesh from the skins. Add the soft pumpkin to the stock pan, discarding the skin. Remove from the heat and blitz the soup with a hand blender until creamy and smooth. Season to taste, adding extra chilli or garam masala if you like. Put back over a low heat and stir in the cream or crème fraîche. If you're not planning to eat all the soup immediately, leave to cool completely, then transfer to a freezerproof container and freeze for up to three months. Defrost in the fridge overnight, then reheat until piping hot before serving.
4. Bring to a gentle simmer, then serve in bowls with a drizzle more cream or crème fraîche and another pinch of chilli to serve, if you like. Any leftovers will keep in the fridge for up to four days.

NUTRITIONAL INFO

PER SERVING KCAL **315** | FAT **24G** | SATURATES **10G** | CARBS **15G** | SUGARS **11G** | FIBRE **8G** | PROTEIN **5G** | SALT **0.59G**

Meat

Sausage Ragu

Prep: 5 mins
Cook: 45 mins

Serves 4

3 tbsp olive oil
1 onion, finely chopped
2 large garlic cloves, crushed
¼ tsp chilli flakes
2 rosemary sprigs, leaves finely chopped
2 x 400g (14oz) cans chopped tomatoes
1 tbsp light brown soft sugar
6 pork sausages
150ml (5fl oz) whole milk
zest of 1 lemon
350g (12oz) dried rigatoni pasta

To serve

grated parmesan
½ small bunch of parsley, leaves roughly chopped

1 Heat 2 tbsp of the oil in a saucepan over a medium heat. Fry the onion with a pinch of salt for 7 mins. Add the garlic, chilli flakes and rosemary and cook for 1 min more. Tip in the tomatoes and sugar. Simmer for 20 mins.

2 Heat the remaining oil in a medium frying pan over a medium heat. Squeeze the sausagemeat from the skins into the pan and fry, breaking it up with a wooden spoon, for 5–7 mins until golden. Add to the sauce along with the milk and lemon zest. Simmer for a further 5 mins. You can now freeze the sauce for another day if you wish. Leave it to cool completely, then transfer to an airtight container and freeze for up to three months. Defrost in the fridge overnight, then reheat until piping hot before continuing.

3 Meanwhile, cook the pasta following pack instructions. Drain and toss with the sauce. Scatter over the parmesan and parsley to serve.

NUTRITIONAL INFO

PER SERVING KCAL **601** | FAT **22G** | SATURATES **7G** | CARBS **73G** | SUGARS **18G** | FIBRE **7G** | PROTEIN **21G** | SALT **1.04G**

✻

Big-Batch Bolognese

Prep: 25 mins
Cook: 1 hr and 30 mins

Serves 12

4 tbsp olive oil
6 smoked bacon rashers, chopped
4 onions, finely chopped
3 carrots, finely chopped
4 celery sticks, finely chopped
8 garlic cloves, crushed
2 tbsp dried mixed herbs
2 bay leaves
500g (1lb 2oz) mushrooms, sliced
1.5kg (3lb 5oz) lean minced beef (or use half minced beef, half minced pork)
6 x 400g (14oz) cans chopped tomatoes
6 tbsp tomato purée
large glass of red wine (optional)
4 tbsp red wine vinegar
1 tbsp sugar

To serve

cooked pasta
shaved parmesan

1 Heat the oil in a very large saucepan. Gently cook the bacon, onions, carrots and celery for 20 mins until golden. Add the garlic, herbs, bay leaves and mushrooms, then cook for 2 mins more.

2 Heat a large frying pan until really hot. Crumble in just enough of the minced meat to cover the pan and cook until brown, then tip in with the veg. Continue to fry the minced meat in batches until it's all cooked. Tip the tomatoes and purée in with the meat and veg. Rinse the cans out with the red wine, if you have some, or with a little water, then add to the pan with the vinegar and sugar. Season generously and bring to a simmer. Simmer slowly for 1 hr until thick and saucy and the minced meat is tender.

3 If you're not planning to eat all the bolognese straight away, leave to cool completely, then divide the sauce into portions in freezerproof containers and freeze. Defrost in the fridge overnight, then reheat until piping hot before serving with pasta and plenty of parmesan.

NUTRITIONAL INFO

PER SERVING KCAL **295** | FAT **12G** | SATURATES **4G** | CARBS **13G** | SUGARS **11G** | FIBRE **4G** | PROTEIN **34G** | SALT **0.87G**

✱

Prep: 20 mins
Cook: 30 mins

Pancetta, Pea & Asparagus Orecchiette Bake

Serves 4

300g (10½oz) dried orecchiette pasta
80g (2¾oz) frozen peas
1 tbsp olive oil
130g (4¾oz) diced pancetta
125g (4½oz) asparagus spears, trimmed and cut into 4
1 garlic clove, finely sliced
75g (2¾oz) butter
75g (2¾oz) plain flour
750ml (1⅓ pints) milk
60g (2¼oz) cheddar, grated
90g (3¼oz) parmesan, grated
20g (¾oz) panko breadcrumbs

1 Bring a saucepan of salted water to the boil. Add the orecchiette and cook for 4 mins less than stated on the pack instructions. Add the peas for the final minute of cooking. Drain and set aside.

2 Heat the oil in a large frying pan over a medium heat. Add the pancetta and fry for about 6 mins until golden. Add the asparagus and garlic and cook for 2–3 mins. Tip everything into a bowl and set aside.

3 Melt the butter in the frying pan. Whisk in the flour and start to add the milk a little at a time, whisking well until you have a creamy sauce. Simmer for 3–4 mins until thickened. Remove from the heat and stir through the cheddar and 60g (2¼oz) of the parmesan. Once melted and smooth, season the sauce to taste. Mix in the cooked pasta and the asparagus mixture. Spoon into an ovenproof dish (approximately 25 x 30cm/10 x 12 inches). Scatter over the breadcrumbs along with the remaining parmesan.

4 If cooking immediately, heat the grill to high. Grill for 5–6 mins until golden and bubbling. Otherwise, leave to cool completely, then cover well before freezing for up to three months. Defrost in the fridge overnight, then heat the oven to 200°C/180°C fan/400°F/Gas Mark 6. Bake for 25 mins until golden. Finish under a hot grill to crisp up the topping.

NUTRITIONAL INFO

PER SERVING KCAL **932** | FAT **48G** | SATURATES **25G** | CARBS **84G** | SUGARS **11G** | FIBRE **7G** | PROTEIN **38G** | SALT **2.2G**

✱

Prep: 20 mins
Cook: 25–30 mins

Sausage & Fennel Meatballs with Creamy Tomato Butter Beans

Serves 4

2 tbsp olive oil
2 garlic cloves, finely sliced
1 tbsp tomato purée
400g (14oz) can chopped tomatoes
2 x 400g (14oz) cans butter beans, drained
400g (14oz) pork sausagemeat or sausages, skins removed
1 tsp fennel seeds
100g (3½oz) ricotta
20g (¾oz) parmesan, grated, plus extra to serve
20g (¾oz) panko breadcrumbs
70ml (2¼oz) double cream
small handful of basil, finely shredded
green salad, to serve

1 Heat the oil in a saucepan over a medium heat. Add the garlic and cook for 1 min before adding the tomato purée. Cook for 1 min, then add the chopped tomatoes, swilling out the can with water and adding that too, then the butter beans. Bring to a simmer and cook for 10 mins.

2 Tip the sausagemeat, fennel seeds, ricotta, parmesan and breadcrumbs into a large bowl and season with pepper. Mix well using your hands, then divide into 12 balls. Remove the sauce from the heat, add the cream and season to taste.

3 Heat the oven to 200°C/180°C fan/400°F/Gas Mark 6. Pour the creamy butter beans into a shallow baking dish and put the meatballs on top. Cook in the oven for 25–30 mins. If you want to save the dish for another day, you can now leave to cool fully, cover well, then freeze for up to three months. Defrost in the fridge overnight, then reheat for another 25–30 mins in the oven at 200°C/180°C fan/400°F/Gas Mark 6.

4 Top with parmesan shavings and the basil. Serve with a green salad.

NUTRITIONAL INFO

PER SERVING KCAL **596** | FAT **39G** | SATURATES **16G** | CARBS **31G** | SUGARS **7G** | FIBRE **10G** | PROTEIN **25G** | SALT **1.6G**

✱

Cottage Pie

Prep: 35 mins
Cook: 1 hr and 50 mins

Serves 10

3 tbsp olive oil
1.25kg (2lb 12oz) minced beef
2 onions, finely chopped
3 carrots, chopped
3 celery sticks, chopped
2 garlic cloves, finely chopped
3 tbsp plain flour
1 tbsp tomato purée
large glass of red wine (optional)
850ml (1½ pints) beef stock
4 tbsp Worcestershire sauce
a few thyme sprigs
2 bay leaves

For the mash

1.8kg (4lb) potatoes, chopped
225ml (8fl oz) milk
25g (1oz) butter
200g (7oz) strong cheddar, grated
freshly grated nutmeg

1 Heat 1 tbsp of the olive oil in a large saucepan and fry the minced beef until browned – you may need to do this in batches. Set the meat aside as it browns.

2 Put the remaining oil into the pan, add the onions, carrots and celery and cook for about 20 mins over a gentle heat until soft. Add the garlic, flour and tomato purée, increase the heat and cook for a few minutes, then return the beef to the pan. Pour over the red wine, if using, and boil to reduce it slightly before adding the stock, Worcestershire sauce, thyme sprigs and bay leaves.

3 Bring to a simmer and cook, uncovered, for 45 mins. By this time the gravy should be thick and coating the meat. Check after about 30 mins – if a lot of liquid remains, increase the heat slightly to reduce the gravy a little. Season well, then discard the bay leaves and thyme stalks.

4 Meanwhile, make the mash. In a large saucepan, cover the chopped potatoes in salted cold water, bring to the boil and simmer until tender. Drain well, then allow to steam-dry for a few minutes. Mash well with the milk, butter and three-quarters of the cheese, then season with freshly grated nutmeg and some salt and pepper.

5 Spoon the meat mixture into two ovenproof dishes. Pipe or spoon on the mash to cover. Sprinkle over the remaining cheese. You can now freeze one portion – leave to cool completely, then wrap well and freeze for up to three months. Always freeze the pie on the day that you make it. Defrost in the fridge overnight, then cook as below.

6 Heat the oven to 220°C/200°C fan/425°F/Gas Mark 7 and cook for 25–30 mins or until the topping is golden.

NUTRITIONAL INFO

PER SERVING KCAL **597** | FAT **34G** | SATURATES **16G** | CARBS **34.06G** | SUGARS **7G** | FIBRE **4G** | PROTEIN **36G** | SALT **0.98G**

Prep: 10 mins
Cook: 30 mins

Spiced Lamb Meatball Stew

Serves 4

1 tbsp oil
12 shop-bought lamb meatballs
1 onion, sliced
2 large garlic cloves, crushed
2 tsp ground cumin
1 tsp ground coriander
½ tsp ground cinnamon
1 tbsp rose harissa
400g (14oz) can chopped tomatoes
200ml (7fl oz) low-salt lamb or beef stock
2 x 400g (14oz) cans chickpeas, drained and rinsed
small bunch of flat-leaf parsley, finely chopped
½ small bunch of mint, chopped
50g (1¾oz) pomegranate seeds

1 Heat the oil in a large, shallow, flameproof casserole dish or deep frying pan. Add the meatballs and fry for 3–4 mins, turning regularly, until golden. Remove and set aside.

2 Tip the onion into the pan and fry for 7 mins until softened. Stir through the garlic, cumin, coriander and cinnamon and cook for 1 min. Add the harissa, tomatoes and stock and bring to a simmer. Stir through the chickpeas and the meatballs, season and simmer for 10–15 mins until slightly reduced and the meatballs are cooked through.

3 If you're not going to eat all the stew now, you can freeze some for another day. Leave to cool completely, then transfer to a freezerproof container and freeze for up to three months. Defrost thoroughly in the fridge overnight, then warm through in a pan over a medium heat for 10–12 mins until the meatballs are piping hot all the way through.

4 Stir through half the herbs, scatter the rest on top along with the pomegranate seeds and serve.

NUTRITIONAL INFO

PER SERVING KCAL **454** | FAT **21G** | SATURATES **6G** | CARBS **35G** | SUGARS **9G** | FIBRE **11G** | PROTEIN **26G** | SALT **1.02G**

✳

Prep: 40 mins
Cook: 4 hrs and 30 mins

Pork, Fennel & Ricotta Lasagne

Serves 10–12

3 tbsp olive oil
100g (3½oz) diced pancetta
1kg (2lb 4oz) minced pork
500g (1lb 2oz) onions, finely sliced
2 celery sticks, finely chopped
3 carrots, finely chopped
1 fennel bulb, around 275g (9¾oz), finely chopped
6 garlic cloves, crushed
5 rosemary sprigs
3 bay leaves
2 tsp fennel seeds (optional)
2 tsp golden caster sugar
200ml (7fl oz) dry white wine
1 litre (1¾ pints) chicken stock
400ml (14fl oz) whole milk
1 tbsp Worcestershire sauce
300g (10½oz) Swiss chard, stalks finely sliced and leaves roughly chopped
500g (1lb 2oz) dried lasagne sheets

For the béchamel

85g (3oz) butter
85g (3oz) plain flour
1 litre (1¾ pints) whole milk
½ whole nutmeg
250g (9oz) ricotta
100g (3½oz) parmesan, grated

NUTRITIONAL INFO

PER SERVING (IF SERVING 12) KCAL **625** | FAT **29G** | SATURATES **14G** | CARBS **49G** | SUGARS **13G** | FIBRE **5G** | PROTEIN **36G** | SALT **1.53G**

1 Add 1 tbsp of the oil to a large, deep, lidded, flameproof casserole dish. Stir in the pancetta and cook over a medium–high heat for 5–6 mins until golden, then transfer to a bowl using a slotted spoon. Add the minced pork to the pan in batches. Brown for about 8 mins, then transfer to the same bowl as the pancetta. Pour in the remaining oil and stir in the onions, celery, carrots, fennel and a pinch of salt. Cook for 10–12 mins, partially covered, until the veg have softened. Stir in the garlic, rosemary, bay leaves, fennel seeds, if using, and sugar, cooking for a few more minutes until fragrant. Return the meat to the dish.

2 Splash in the white wine and reduce by half. Pour in the stock, milk and Worcestershire sauce. Bring to the boil, then place the lid on slightly askew and set the heat to a simmer. Cook for 3½ hrs.

3 Stir in the chard stalks. Cook for a further 30 mins until reduced but there is still some liquid and the flavours have developed. Stir in the chard leaves and season to taste. Once cooled completely, you can keep the ragu in the fridge, covered, for up to three days.

4 To make the béchamel, heat the butter in a large saucepan over a medium heat until foaming. Stir in the flour and cook for 2–3 mins until darkened. Splash in the milk, a little at a time, whisking well, making sure you get right into the corner of the pan. Once all the milk has been added, grate in the nutmeg and bring to a gentle simmer. Cook, stirring frequently, for 4–5 mins until thickened, then remove from the heat and whisk in the ricotta and half the parmesan. Season well and set aside.

5 To assemble the lasagne, remove and discard the rosemary sprigs and bay leaves from the ragu. Spread two ladles of béchamel over the base of a large baking dish, then top with three ladles of ragu, spreading this right out to the edges too, then a layer of lasagne sheets. Repeat this process to make about five layers, finishing with the final two ladles of béchamel. Scatter over the remaining parmesan. Season well with pepper. Alternatively, divide the lasagne between two heatproof, freezerproof dishes so that you can freeze one for another time.

6 The lasagne will now keep chilled for up to one day or wrapped in the freezer for up to three months. Leave to cool completely and defrost in the fridge overnight before cooking. To cook, heat the oven to 200°C/180°C fan/400°F/Gas Mark 6. Bake for 30–40 mins, or 40–50 mins if cooking from chilled, until the edges are crispy.

✳

Prep: 30 mins
Cook: 3 hrs and 30 mins

Stout-Braised Short Ribs with Horseradish & Carrots

Serves 4

2 tbsp sunflower oil
4 short ribs on the bone
1 onion, chopped
3 celery sticks, chopped
4 bay leaves
1 tbsp dried mixed herbs
1 tbsp plain flour
2 tbsp light brown soft sugar
500ml (18fl oz) stout
300ml (10fl oz) beef stock
3 tbsp horseradish cream
4 carrots, peeled but left whole

1 Heat the oven to 160°C/140°C fan/325°F/Gas Mark 3. Heat the oil in a lidded, flameproof casserole dish and brown the short ribs well on all sides – this will take about 10 mins. Remove the ribs to a plate, then fry the onion and celery for 5 mins. Stir in the bay leaves, herbs and flour and cook for a few minutes, then stir in the sugar, stout and stock. Bring to a simmer. Add the horseradish cream and some seasoning, then nestle the ribs into the sauce. Cover and cook in the oven for 1 hr.

2 Remove the stew from the oven, stir gently and add the whole carrots. Cover and return to the oven for 2 hrs more until the ribs are tender. You can now serve the stew, rustic style, as is. Alternatively, gently remove the ribs and carrots to a board. Strain the sauce through a sieve into a saucepan and bring to the boil, skimming off any froth that rises to the surface. Simmer for 5 mins until reduced by a third. Tip the reduced sauce back into the casserole dish, add the ribs and carrots back in and simmer for a few minutes to reheat the meat. Divide between plates and serve. Any leftovers keep extremely well in the fridge for up to three days or in the freezer for up to two months.

NUTRITIONAL INFO
PER SERVING KCAL **611** | FAT **36G** | SATURATES **9G** | CARBS **29G** | SUGARS **23G** | FIBRE **4G** | PROTEIN **35G** | SALT **0.7G**

Lemongrass & Lime Pork Meatballs with Pickled Veg

Prep: 25 mins
Cook: 15 mins

Serves 4

For the meatballs

1 lime, zested, the lime then cut into wedges

25g (1oz) coriander, finely chopped

1 tbsp fish sauce

1–2 tbsp sriracha, to taste, plus extra for serving (optional)

3 tbsp lemongrass paste

2 spring onions, finely sliced

3 garlic cloves, crushed

1 tbsp golden caster sugar

1 tbsp cornflour

500g (1lb 2 oz) minced pork

1 tbsp vegetable oil

For the pickled veg

2 tbsp rice wine vinegar

1 tbsp golden caster sugar

250g (9oz) carrots, peeled into ribbons or cut into matchsticks

1 cucumber, deseeded and peeled into ribbons or cut into matchsticks

To serve

cooked sticky rice or crusty baguettes

1 First make the pickled veg. Stir the vinegar and sugar together in a small bowl until the sugar has dissolved. Season with a pinch of salt and stir in the carrots and cucumber. Set aside.

2 Tip all the ingredients for the meatballs, except the oil, into a bowl along with a pinch of salt and pepper. Scrunch the mixture together using your hands until everything is well combined. Roll into 20 small balls, around 30g (1oz) each. Heat the oil in a frying pan over a medium–high heat. Add the meatballs and cook all over for 8–10 mins until dark brown and cooked through.

3 Serve over sticky rice alongside the lime wedges for squeezing over, a little more sriracha, if you like, and the pickled veg. You can keep some meatballs aside in the fridge to pile into a crusty baguette the next day.

NUTRITIONAL INFO

PER SERVING KCAL **320** | FAT **14G** | SATURATES **4G** | CARBS **22G** | SUGARS **17G** | FIBRE **4G** | PROTEIN **25G** | SALT **1.5G**

✻

Prep: 15 mins
Cook: 35 mins

Meatballs in Tomato, Cardamom & Lime Sauce

Serves 4

400g (14oz) 15%-fat minced beef
20g (¾oz) dill, roughly chopped
½ tsp bicarbonate of soda
3 tbsp olive oil
2 shallots, finely chopped
3 garlic cloves, finely chopped
1 green chilli, finely chopped
1 tbsp tomato purée
2 x 400g (14oz) cans chopped tomatoes
2 tsp ground cardamom or 12 cardamom pods, opened and crushed
zest and juice of 1 lime
1 tsp sugar, plus an extra pinch
flatbreads or cooked couscous or rice, to serve

1. Mix together the minced beef, half the dill, the bicarbonate of soda (to help keep the meatballs juicy) and plenty of salt and pepper in a bowl. Roll into roughly 20 meatballs (about 25g/1oz each), then put them in the fridge while you make the sauce.
2. Heat 2 tbsp of the oil in a large, shallow, lidded pan over a medium–low heat. Add the shallots, garlic, chilli and a pinch of salt and cook for 8–10 mins until the shallots are lightly caramelized.
3. Add the tomato purée and turn up the heat slightly. Cook for 2–3 mins until it has darkened. Add the chopped tomatoes, 150ml (5fl oz) water, the cardamom, lime zest, sugar and a good pinch of salt. Bring to the boil, then reduce the heat to a simmer and cook for 10 mins. Heat the grill to high.
4. Tip the meatballs into the sauce, cover the pan and cook for 8–10 mins until they are nearly cooked through. Remove the lid, then put the pan under the grill for 4–5 mins until the top has some colour. Remove from the grill and leave to cool slightly. Once they are cool, the meatballs and sauce will keep chilled for up to two days and frozen for up to three months.
5. To serve, mix the rest of the dill with the lime juice, remaining oil, an extra pinch of sugar and some seasoning. Dot this over the meatballs, then serve with flatbreads, couscous or rice.

NUTRITIONAL INFO

PER SERVING KCAL **362** | FAT **25G** | SATURATES **8G** | CARBS **10G** | SUGARS **10G** | FIBRE **3G** | PROTEIN **23G** | SALT **0.6G**

✱

Prep: 15 mins
Cook: 4 hrs

Feed-A-Crowd Lamb Stew

Serves 8

1.5kg (3lb 5oz) boneless lamb shoulder, cut into large chunks
50g (1¾oz) plain flour
2 tbsp vegetable oil
2 onions, roughly chopped
6 large carrots, halved lengthways and thickly sliced
2 garlic cloves, finely chopped
2 tbsp tomato purée
1.2 litres (2 pints) lamb or chicken stock
2 bay leaves
large rosemary sprig or a pinch of dried rosemary

To serve (optional)
mashed potato
cooked green beans

1. Put the lamb and flour in a bowl, season and toss to coat. Heat the oil in a large frying pan or flameproof casserole dish over a medium heat, then fry in batches for 5–8 mins until browned all over. Tip the meat into your slow cooker.
2. Add the onions and carrots and cook for 5–8 mins until starting to colour, then stir in the garlic and cook for 1 min more. Scatter in any leftover flour and stir for 1 min. Stir in the tomato purée and cook for a few minutes more.
3. Pour the stock over the veg, stir and bring to the boil. Pour over the lamb. Nestle in the bay leaves and rosemary, season and cook on high for 3–4 hrs, medium for 5–6 hrs or low for 7 hrs, stirring occasionally, until the lamb is tender.
4. If not eating immediately, or if you have leftovers, let the stew cool completely. It can then be frozen for up to three months. Defrost thoroughly in the fridge overnight and reheat in a pan until piping hot. Serve with mash and green beans, if you like.

NUTRITIONAL INFO
PER SERVING KCAL **554** | FAT **36G** | SATURATES **15G** | CARBS **13G** | SUGARS **7G** | FIBRE **3G** | PROTEIN **43G** | SALT **0.4G**

✱

Pulled Pork

Prep: 15 mins
Cook: 4–8 hrs

Serves 12

2 tsp smoked paprika
2 tsp ground cumin
2 tsp black pepper
2 tsp light brown soft sugar
1 tsp salt
about 2.5kg (5lb 8oz) boneless pork shoulder joint
2 medium mugfuls of cider, plus extra if needed
1 mugful of good, smoky barbecue sauce

To serve (optional)

soft white rolls
coleslaw

TIP

Try serving this with the Tangy Cabbage Coleslaw on page 194.

1. Preheat the oven to 150°C/130°C fan/300°F/Gas Mark 2. Mix together the smoked paprika, ground cumin, pepper, sugar and salt. Rub all over the pork.
2. Put the pork in a large, lidded casserole dish, skin-side up, and pour over the cider. Cover and cook for 4–8 hours until the meat is falling apart. Check every few hours in case it gets dry – if it does, add another mugful of cider.
3. Remove the casserole dish from the oven and transfer the meat to a big dish, leaving the liquid in the casserole. Cut the skin off, then shred the meat using two forks, ditching any fatty bits. Skim any excess fat off the surface of the sauce.
4. Add the barbecue sauce to the liquid in the casserole dish, mix it in, then ladle some into a bowl for dipping.
5. Put the pulled pork back into the casserole dish, along with its juices so that it stays moist. Season to taste. Once cool, you can keep the meat in the fridge, covered, for up to 24 hrs until you're ready to serve. Alternatively, transfer to a freezerproof container and freeze for up to three months. Defrost in the fridge overnight before serving.
6. Serve the pulled pork in soft white rolls with coleslaw, with the bowl of sauce on the side for dipping your sandwiches into while you're eating.

NUTRITIONAL INFO

PER SERVING KCAL **383** | FAT **24G** | SATURATES **8G** | CARBS **5G** | SUGARS **5G** | FIBRE **0G** | PROTEIN **38G** | SALT **0.8G**

Traybake Lamb Kebab with Spinach Sauce

Prep: 25 mins
Cook: 30 mins

Serves 4 plus leftovers

- 1 tbsp sunflower oil, plus extra for the tin
- 3 roasted red peppers from a jar, drained
- 1 onion, roughly chopped
- 3 garlic cloves, roughly chopped
- small handful of parsley, roughly chopped
- 2 tsp ground cumin
- 1 tbsp tomato purée
- 1 tsp pul biber (optional)
- 800g (1lb 12oz) minced lamb
- flatbreads, to serve

For the yogurt sauce

- 260g (9¼oz) spinach
- 2 small garlic cloves, crushed
- 400ml (14fl oz) Greek-style natural yogurt
- 1 tbsp tahini
- ½ tbsp lemon juice

For the salad

- 1 cucumber, deseeded and finely chopped
- 1 red onion, finely sliced
- 4 long pickled green chillies, finely sliced (optional)
- juice of 1 lemon
- small handful of parsley, finely chopped
- 3 tbsp extra virgin olive oil

1. To make the yogurt sauce, boil a kettle full of water and tip the spinach into a colander or sieve. Pour the boiling water over the spinach and set aside to cool. Once cool enough to handle, squeeze out as much moisture as you can with your hands, then roughly chop and tip into a bowl. Mix in all the other ingredients and season to taste. Cover and set aside in the fridge until needed.
2. Heat the oven to 240°C/220°C fan/475°F/Gas Mark 9. Brush a 20cm (8 inch) square cake tin with a little oil. Tip the peppers, onion, garlic, parsley, cumin, tomato purée, pul biber, if using, and 1½ tsp salt into a food processor. Blitz until finely chopped, then add the lamb and keep blitzing until very well combined. Pat the kebab mixture into the oiled tin. Brush over the 1 tbsp oil and roast in the oven for 15 mins until browned around the edges or until a digital cooking thermometer reads 75°C (167°F) when pushed into the middle.
3. Heat the grill to high and cook for a further 5–10 mins until cooked all the way through. If not eating immediately, leave the traybake kebab to cool. It will keep chilled for up to two days and is perfect for flavour-packed on-the-go lunches.
4. Meanwhile, mix all the salad ingredients together and season to taste. Cut the kebab into slices and serve on a platter with the salad, sauce and flatbreads on the side so that everyone can help themselves.

NUTRITIONAL INFO

PER SERVING KCAL **641** | FAT **45G** | SATURATES **19G** | CARBS **14G** | SUGARS **11G** | FIBRE **4G** | PROTEIN **43G** | SALT **1.46G**

✳

Prep: 10 mins
Cook: 45 mins

Carbonara Cacio & Pepe Mac & Cheese

Serves 4 plus leftovers

- 50g (1¾oz) butter, plus extra for the dish
- 150g (5½oz) diced smoked pancetta
- 1 tsp cracked black pepper
- 50g (1¾oz) plain flour
- 700ml (1¼ pints) whole milk
- 350g (12oz) dried macaroni
- 150g (5½oz) extra-mature cheddar, grated
- 50g (1¾oz) parmesan, finely grated
- 50g (1¾oz) grated mozzarella
- 50g (1¾oz) panko breadcrumbs

1. Melt the butter in a saucepan over a medium heat until sizzling, then fry the pancetta for 5–6 mins until crisp and golden. Turn the heat down to low, add the black pepper and cook for 2 mins until well toasted. Stir in the flour and cook for 1 min more, then gradually whisk in the milk until smooth. Simmer for 3–4 mins, stirring until thickened.
2. Meanwhile, cook the macaroni following pack instructions until al dente, then drain. Take the sauce off the heat and stir through the cheddar and half the parmesan until melted and smooth. Taste and season if needed, then mix in the pasta. At the last minute, stir through the mozzarella.
3. Butter an 18 x 25cm (7 x 10 inch) ovenproof dish. Spoon in the pasta and smooth the top. Scatter over the breadcrumbs and remaining Parmesan. Once cool, you can freeze your pasta bake for up to one month. Defrost thoroughly in the fridge overnight before continuing.
4. Heat the oven to 200°C/180°C fan/400°F/Gas Mark 6. Bake your mac and cheese for 30 mins until golden on top and bubbling and piping hot throughout.

NUTRITIONAL INFO

PER SERVING KCAL **980** | FAT **49G** | SATURATES **27G** | CARBS **89G** | SUGARS **10G** | FIBRE **5G** | PROTEIN **42G** | SALT **2.72G**

Chicken & Turkey

Chicken Enchiladas

Prep: 20 mins
Cook: 50 mins

Serves 10

3 tbsp olive oil
2 red onions, sliced
2 red peppers, sliced
3 red chillies, 2 deseeded and chopped, 1 sliced
small bunch of coriander, stalks finely chopped, leaves roughly chopped, plus extra to serve (optional)
2 garlic cloves, crushed
1 tbsp ground coriander
1 tbsp cumin seeds
6 chicken breasts, cut into small chunks
415g (14¾oz) can refried beans
198g (7oz) can sweetcorn, drained
700ml (1¼ pints) passata
1 tsp golden caster sugar
10 tortillas (flour or corn)
280ml (9½fl oz) soured cream
200g (7oz) cheddar, grated

1. Heat 2 tbsp of the oil in a large pan, then fry the onions, peppers, chopped chillies and coriander stalks with 1 crushed garlic clove for 10 mins until soft. Stir in 2 tsp of the ground coriander and 2 tsp of the cumin seeds, then fry for 1 min more.
2. Meanwhile, in another frying pan, fry the chicken in the remaining oil, in batches, until browned. Add it to the pan of veg as it is done.
3. Stir the refried beans, sweetcorn, coriander leaves and 150ml (5fl oz) of the passata into the veg and chicken. In a bowl, mix the rest of the passata with the other crushed garlic clove, the remaining spices and the sugar, then set aside.
4. To assemble, lay the tortillas (you can warm them quickly in the microwave to make them more pliable if you like) onto a board and divide the chicken mixture between them, folding over the ends and rolling up to seal. Divide the passata sauce into your chosen dish(es) – you can use a metal dish or smaller individual foil or metal dishes if you're going to freeze this. Top with the enchiladas. Dot over the soured cream, sprinkle with the grated cheese and scatter with the sliced chilli.
5. If eating straight away, heat the oven to 200°C/180°C fan/400°F/Gas Mark 6, then cook for 30 mins. Scatter the enchiladas with more coriander leaves before serving, if you like.
6. Alternatively, cool completely, cover and freeze for up to one month. Defrost in the fridge overnight. Heat the oven to 160°C/140°C fan/325°F/Gas Mark 3 and cook, covered with foil, for 1 hr. Increase the heat to 200°C/180°C fan/400°F/Gas Mark 6, remove the foil and cook for a further 15–20 mins until bubbling and delicious.

NUTRITIONAL INFO

PER SERVING KCAL **468** | FAT **20G** | SATURATES **10G** | CARBS **36G** | SUGARS **10G** | FIBRE **6G** | PROTEIN **33G** | SALT **1.7G**

✱

Prep: 10 mins
Cook: 40 mins

Peanut Butter Chicken

Serves 4

2 tbsp avocado oil
8 chicken thigh fillets, cut into chunks
1 onion, finely chopped
3 garlic cloves, crushed
2 red chillies, finely sliced (deseeded if you don't like it too hot)
2 tsp grated ginger
2 tbsp garam masala
100g (3½oz) smooth peanut butter
400ml (14fl oz) can coconut milk
400g (14oz) can chopped tomatoes
bunch of coriander, half roughly chopped, half leaves picked

To serve

handful of roasted peanuts
cooked rice

1 Heat 1 tbsp of the oil in a deep frying pan over a medium heat. Brown the chicken in batches, setting aside once golden. Fry the onion for 8 mins until softened. Then add the garlic, chillies and ginger and fry in the remaining oil for 1 min. Add the garam masala and fry for 1 min more.

2 Stir in the peanut butter, coconut milk and tomatoes and bring to a simmer. Return the chicken to the pan and add the chopped coriander. Cook for 30 mins until the sauce thickens and the chicken is cooked through. If not eating immediately, or if you have leftovers, let it cool completely. It can then be frozen for up to two months. Defrost thoroughly in the fridge overnight and reheat in a pan until piping hot.

3 Serve scattered with the coriander leaves and the roasted peanuts, with some rice on the side.

NUTRITIONAL INFO

PER SERVING KCAL **579** | FAT **43G** | SATURATES **20G** | CARBS **12G** | SUGARS **6G** | FIBRE **3G** | PROTEIN **32G** | SALT **0.3G**

✱

Prep: 20 mins
Cook: 1 hr and 30 mins

One-Pot Chicken Chasseur

Serves 4

1 tsp olive oil
25g (1oz) butter
4 chicken legs
1 onion, chopped
2 garlic cloves, crushed
200g (7oz) small button or chestnut mushrooms
225ml (8fl oz) red wine
2 tbsp tomato purée
2 thyme sprigs
500ml (18fl oz) chicken stock

1 Heat the oil and half the butter in a large, lidded, flameproof casserole dish. Season the chicken legs, then fry for about 5 mins on each side until golden brown. Remove and set aside.

2 Melt the remaining butter in the pan, add the onion and fry for about 5 mins until soft. Add the garlic and cook for 1 min more. Add the mushrooms and cook for 2 mins, then add the red wine. Stir in the tomato purée and let the liquid bubble and reduce for about 5 mins. Then add the thyme sprigs, pour over the stock and stir.

3 Slip the chicken legs back into the pan, then cover and simmer on a low heat for about 1 hr until the chicken is very tender.

4 Remove the chicken legs from the pan and keep warm. Rapidly boil down the sauce for 10 mins or so until it is syrupy and the flavour has concentrated. Put the chicken legs back into the sauce and serve.

5 If not eating immediately, or if you have leftovers, leave to cool completely, then portion into freezerproof containers. Freeze for up to three months. Defrost in the fridge overnight, then reheat over a low heat until piping hot all the way through. The sauce may need a splash of water to help bring it back.

NUTRITIONAL INFO

PER SERVING KCAL **439** | FAT **28G** | SATURATES **10G** | CARBS **7G** | SUGARS **6G** | FIBRE **2G** | PROTEIN **35G** | SALT **1.11G**

✻

Prep: 10 mins
Cook: 1 hr

Pulled Chicken & Black Bean Chilli

Serves 8

4 tbsp sunflower oil
4 onions, sliced
8 chicken thigh fillets
6 garlic cloves, finely chopped
pinch of golden caster sugar
2 tbsp dried oregano
2 tsp cumin seeds
2 tsp chipotle paste
700ml (1¼ pints) passata
1 chicken stock cube
2 x 400g (14oz) cans black beans, drained
juice of 1 lime
tortillas or cooked rice, to serve

To serve (optional)

coriander
crumbled feta
lime wedges
chopped red onion

1 Heat the oil in a shallow, lidded saucepan or flameproof casserole dish. Tip in the onions and cook over a medium–low heat for 5 mins until softened. Add the chicken and turn up the heat to medium. Stir in the garlic, sugar, oregano, cumin seeds and some seasoning. Cook for a couple of minutes, then add the chipotle paste and cook for a few minutes more. Pour in the passata and 200ml (7fl oz) water and crumble in the stock cube. Season, stir and bring to a simmer.

2 Cover with the lid and cook for 40–50 mins, stirring occasionally, until the chicken is tender. Shred the chicken into the sauce using two forks, then stir through the black beans. Simmer for 5 mins more, then turn off the heat. Squeeze in the lime juice. If not eating immediately, or if you have leftovers, let the chilli cool completely. It can then be frozen for up to two months. Defrost thoroughly in the fridge overnight and reheat in a pan until piping hot.

3 Serve with tortillas or rice, and some coriander, feta, lime wedges and red onion on the side, if you like.

NUTRITIONAL INFO

PER SERVING KCAL **256** | FAT **10G** | SATURATES **2G** | CARBS **18G** | SUGARS **8G** | FIBRE **7G** | PROTEIN **19G** | SALT **0.9G**

✳

Prep: 20 mins
Cook: 2 hrs

Spring Green Chicken Stew with Cheddar Dumplings

Serves 4

2 tbsp olive oil
8 chicken thigh fillets
100g (3½oz) smoked bacon lardons, diced pancetta or chopped bacon
1 large onion, chopped
1 leek, chopped
2 garlic cloves, crushed
2 tbsp plain flour
100ml (3½fl oz) white wine
500ml (18fl oz) chicken stock
2 bay leaves
100g (3½oz) fresh pesto
small bunch of basil
80g (2¾oz) watercress
100g (3½oz) frozen peas

For the dumplings

125g (4½oz) butter, cut into small pieces
200g (7oz) self-raising flour
75g (2¾oz) extra-mature cheddar, grated

1 Heat the oil in a large, lidded, flameproof casserole dish over a medium–high heat and brown the chicken thighs on all sides until golden all over. You may have to do this in batches. Remove to a plate and set aside.

2 Fry the lardons, pancetta or bacon in the dish for a few minutes, then add the onion and leek. Cook over a medium heat for 8–10 mins until the vegetables have softened. Stir in the garlic and cook for another minute, then add the flour. Season and cook for 2 mins more.

3 Slowly stir in the wine and cook until it has bubbled away, then stir in the stock. Return the chicken to the dish along with the bay leaves and cover with the lid. Reduce the heat to a simmer and cook for 45 mins–1 hr or until the chicken is tender. If not eating that day, let the stew cool completely. It can then be frozen for up to three months. Defrost thoroughly in the fridge overnight and reheat in a pan before continuing.

4 Put the pesto, most of the basil, the watercress and a ladleful of hot liquid from the dish in a food processor or blender. Blitz to a loose green paste, pour into the stew and add the peas. Remove from the heat.

5 Heat the oven to 200°C/180°C fan/400°F/Gas Mark 6. To make the dumplings, rub the butter into the flour in a bowl until it resembles fine breadcrumbs. Mix in half the grated cheese and some seasoning, then add 110ml (3¾fl oz) water, mixing it in using a cutlery knife to form a light, sticky dough. Break off walnut-sized lumps of the dough and shape into small balls.

6 Put the dumplings on top of the stew, then scatter over the remaining cheese. Transfer the dish to the oven for 25 mins until the dumplings are golden brown and cooked through. Scatter over the remaining basil and serve straight away.

NUTRITIONAL INFO

PER SERVING KCAL **1022** | FAT **65G** | SATURATES **28G** | CARBS **57G** | SUGARS **8G** | FIBRE **7G** | PROTEIN **46G** | SALT **3.44G**

✻

Prep: 20 mins
Cook: 1 hr and 5 mins

Chicken, Ham & Leek Pie

Serves 6–8

- 1 tbsp vegetable oil
- 600g (1lb 5oz) chicken thigh fillets, roughly chopped
- 60g (2¼oz) butter
- 2 leeks (about 400g/14oz), sliced
- 2 garlic cloves, finely chopped or grated
- 125ml (4fl oz) white wine
- 60g (2¼oz) plain flour, plus extra for dusting
- 400ml (14fl oz) chicken stock
- 250ml (9fl oz) milk
- 2 bay leaves
- a few thyme sprigs
- 180g (6¼oz) ham (either thick sliced or leftover cooked ham), roughly chopped
- 500g (1lb 2oz) block of puff pastry
- 1 egg, beaten

1 Heat the oil in a large frying pan or saucepan over a medium heat and fry the chicken for 6–8 mins until browned all over (it doesn't need to be cooked through at this point). Remove the chicken to a plate, leaving the oil in the pan.

2 Tip the butter into the pan and fry the leeks for 8–10 mins over a medium–low heat until softened but not golden. Stir in the garlic. Cook for 1 min more. Pour in the white wine and cook for a few minutes so that the alcohol evaporates and the liquid reduces a little.

3 Sprinkle over the flour and stir until a thick paste has formed and no dry flour remains. Gradually pour in the stock, stirring well between each addition until combined – this will take about 5 mins. Pour in the milk, then bring to a simmer and cook for 1 min, stirring constantly to prevent lumps forming.

4 Stir in the bay leaves, thyme, browned chicken and ham. Season with lots of freshly ground black pepper and a pinch of salt (the stock and ham will add salt, so season to taste). You can now keep the pie filling in the fridge for up to two days or in the freezer for up to three months, leaving it to cool completely first. Defrost thoroughly in the fridge overnight before continuing.

5 Heat the oven to 200°C/180°C fan/400°F/Gas Mark 6. Pour your pie filling into a large pie dish (about 20 x 30cm/8 x 12 inches). Lightly dust the work surface with flour, then roll out the puff pastry to 5mm (¼ inch) thickness. Cut a rectangle of pastry big enough to cover the pie dish with a little overhang. Lightly brush the rim of the pie dish with some of the beaten egg, then lay the pastry over the filling and the rim of the dish. Crimp the edges and use any pastry offcuts to decorate the pie, if you like, using a little more beaten egg to help them stick. Glaze the whole pastry top with more beaten egg and cut a steam hole in the centre. Bake for 45 mins–1 hr until golden and the filling is piping hot.

NUTRITIONAL INFO

PER SERVING (IF SERVING 8) KCAL **533** | FAT **32G** | SATURATES **15G** | CARBS **29G** | SUGARS **4G** | FIBRE **4G** | PROTEIN **27G** | SALT **1.7G**

Chicken Nuggets

Prep: 20 mins
Cook: 10–15 mins

Serves 4

400g (14oz) chicken breasts, cut into bite-size pieces
4 tbsp plain flour
1 egg, lightly beaten
115g (4oz) panko breadcrumbs or other dried breadcrumbs
1–2 tbsp oil
ketchup, to serve (optional)

1. Place the chicken pieces between two layers of baking parchment. Use a rolling pin to flatten the pieces gently until they are around 2–3mm (1⁄16–⅛ inch) thick and uniform in size and thickness.
2. Heat the oven to 220°C/200°C fan/425°F/Gas Mark 7. Tip the flour onto a plate and mix it with a pinch of salt. Put the beaten egg in a bowl and tip the breadcrumbs into another bowl.
3. To assemble your nuggets, dip each chicken piece in the flour, then into the egg (shaking off any excess) and finally toss in the breadcrumbs. Using just one hand for the breadcrumbs is less messy. You can now freeze the nuggets – open-freeze on a tray until solid, then transfer to a freezerproof container. Defrost in the fridge overnight before cooking.
4. Transfer the coated chicken pieces to a baking tray brushed with the oil. Cook the nuggets in the oven for 10–15 mins until cooked through, turning them halfway. Serve the chicken nuggets with ketchup, if you like.

NUTRITIONAL INFO

PER SERVING KCAL **337** | FAT **8G** | SATURATES **2G** | CARBS **36G** | SUGARS **1G** | FIBRE **2G** | PROTEIN **30G** | SALT **0.61G**

Chicken & Chorizo Jambalaya

Prep: 10 mins
Cook: 45 mins

Serves 4

1 tbsp olive oil
2 chicken breasts, chopped
1 onion, finely chopped
1 red pepper, thinly sliced
2 garlic cloves, crushed
75g (2¾oz) chorizo, sliced
1 tbsp Cajun seasoning
250g (9oz) long-grain rice
400g (14oz) can plum tomatoes
350ml (12fl oz) chicken stock

1. Heat the oil in a large, lidded, flameproof casserole dish or frying pan over a medium–high heat. Brown the chicken for 5–8 mins until golden. Remove and set aside.
2. Tip in the onion and cook for 3–4 mins until soft. Add the red pepper, garlic, chorizo and Cajun seasoning and cook for 5 mins more.
3. Stir the chicken back in, along with the rice, tomatoes and stock. Cover and simmer over a medium heat for 20–25 mins until the rice is tender. Once cool, you can keep any leftovers in the fridge for up to 24 hrs – reheat thoroughly in a pan, adding a splash of water if needed.

NUTRITIONAL INFO

PER SERVING KCAL **445** | FAT **10G** | SATURATES **3G** | CARBS **64G** | SUGARS **7G** | FIBRE **2G** | PROTEIN **30G** | SALT **1.2G**

✻

Prep: 20 mins
Cook: 1 hr and 25 mins

Chicken, Spinach & Bacon Alfredo Pasta Bake

Serves 6

- 6 smoked streaky bacon rashers
- 1 tbsp olive oil
- 4 chicken thigh fillets
- ½ tsp dried oregano
- 3 garlic cloves, crushed
- 1 chicken stock cube
- 1 heaped tbsp plain flour
- 300ml (10fl oz) double cream
- 500g (1lb 2oz) dried short pasta (we used rigatoni)
- 100g (3½oz) parmesan, grated
- 2 tsp Dijon mustard
- 100g (3½oz) baby spinach, roughly chopped
- large handful of fresh or dried breadcrumbs
- 3 tomatoes, chopped

1. Heat the grill to high. Put the bacon rashers on a baking tray lined with foil and grill for 5 mins on each side until crisp. Leave to cool, then roughly chop.
2. Heat the oil in a large, lidded saucepan or high-sided frying pan over a high heat. Season the chicken thighs, then add them to the pan and brown on both sides. Sprinkle over the oregano and add the garlic, then stir for another minute. Crumble in the stock cube and add 250ml (9fl oz) water. Bring to a simmer, cover and reduce the heat to low–medium. Cook for 15–20 mins until the chicken is tender, topping up with more water if the pan looks dry. Transfer the chicken to a board using tongs, then shred using two forks. Return the shredded chicken to the pan with the sauce.
3. Whisk the flour into the cooking juices in the pan, turn up the heat and keep stirring until you have a smooth paste that clings to the chicken. Add 500ml (18fl oz) water and the cream and bring to a simmer, stirring occasionally, for 8–10 mins or until the sauce has thickened.
4. Meanwhile, cook the pasta in a large pan of salted boiling water for about 10 mins until it is just cooked but retains some bite. Drain.
5. Add most of the parmesan, the mustard, spinach and half the chopped bacon to the sauce, then season to taste, if needed. Stir until the spinach has wilted, then stir in the cooked pasta.
6. Tip the mixture into a large baking dish. Mix the breadcrumbs with the remaining parmesan and scatter over the top along with the tomatoes and remaining chopped bacon. If you want to eat this another day, you can now freeze the cooled pasta dish, wrapped in a double layer of foil, for up to two months. Defrost in the fridge overnight (for at least 10 hrs), then cook as below, adding 5–10 mins to the cooking time.
7. To cook straight away, heat the oven to 200°C/180°C fan/400°F/ Gas Mark 6. Bake for 35–40 mins or until the top is golden and crunchy and the sauce is bubbling.

NUTRITIONAL INFO

PER SERVING KCAL **757** | FAT **43G** | SATURATES **23G** | CARBS **60G** | SUGARS **4G** | FIBRE **5G** | PROTEIN **30G** | SALT **1.9G**

Crispy Sesame Lemon Chicken

Prep: 10 mins
Cook: 15 mins

Serves 6

2 tbsp cornflour
5 tbsp plain flour
1 tsp baking powder
large pinch of white pepper
1 egg, beaten
600g (1lb 5oz) chicken breasts, cut into 2cm (¾ inch) pieces
2 tbsp sunflower or vegetable oil

For the sauce

2 tsp cornflour
zest and juice of 2 lemons
2 tbsp honey
2 tbsp soy sauce
2 tsp sesame seeds
2 tsp sesame oil

To serve

2 spring onions, finely sliced
cooked noodles

1 To make the sauce, tip the cornflour into a bowl and whisk in the lemon zest and juice until any lumps disappear. Add the honey, soy sauce, sesame seeds and sesame oil and mix again. Set aside.

2 For the chicken coating, mix together the cornflour, flour, baking powder, white pepper and beaten egg with ¼ tsp salt and 4 tbsp water in a large bowl. Tip in the chicken pieces, gently tossing to coat.

3 Heat the oil in a large frying pan over a high heat and fry the coated chicken pieces in batches for 6 mins per batch until golden and cooked through. Remove the cooked chicken and transfer to a plate or tray lined with kitchen paper.

4 When all the chicken has been cooked, return it all to the pan, still over a high heat. Immediately pour in the sauce and toss to coat – the sauce will thicken and cling to the chicken. Scatter the spring onions over and serve with noodles.

5 Any leftover chicken will keep in the fridge for up to three days. Reheat over a low heat with a generous splash of water until piping hot all the way through.

NUTRITIONAL INFO

PER SERVING KCAL **280** | FAT **8G** | SATURATES **1G** | CARBS **26G** | SUGARS **7G** | FIBRE **1G** | PROTEIN **26G** | SALT **1.05G**

Turkey Meatloaf

Prep: 15 mins
Cook: 55 mins

Serves 4

1 tbsp olive oil
1 large onion, finely chopped
1 garlic clove, crushed
2 tbsp Worcestershire sauce
2 tsp tomato purée, plus 1 tbsp for the beans
500g (1lb 2oz) minced turkey (thigh is best)
1 large egg, beaten
85g (3oz) fresh white breadcrumbs
2 tbsp barbecue sauce, plus 4 tbsp for the beans
2 x 400g (14oz) cans cannellini beans
1–2 tbsp roughly chopped parsley

1 Heat the oven to 180°C/160°C fan/350°F/Gas Mark 4. Heat the oil in a large frying pan and cook the onion for 8–10 mins until softened. Add the garlic, Worcestershire sauce and the 2 tsp tomato purée and stir until combined. Set aside to cool.

2 Put the minced turkey, beaten egg, breadcrumbs and cooled onion mixture in a large bowl and season well. Mix everything to combine, then shape into a rectangular loaf and place in a large baking dish or roasting tin. Spread the 2 tbsp barbecue sauce over the meatloaf and cook for 30 mins.

3 Meanwhile, drain one can of the beans, then pour both cans into a large bowl. Add the remaining barbecue sauce and tomato purée. Season and set aside.

4 When the meatloaf has had its initial cooking time, scatter the beans around the outside and return to the oven for 15 mins more until the meatloaf is cooked through and the beans are piping hot. Scatter over the parsley and serve the meatloaf in slices.

5 You can freeze any leftovers – leave to cool completely, then divide the meatloaf slices into freezerproof containers, along with the beans. Freeze for up to three months. Defrost in the fridge overnight, then tip into a baking dish, cover with foil and warm through in the oven at to 180°C/160°C fan/350°F/Gas Mark 4 for 30 mins or until piping hot.

NUTRITIONAL INFO

PER SERVING KCAL **416** | FAT **6G** | SATURATES **1G** | CARBS **45G** | SUGARS **11G** | FIBRE **3G** | PROTEIN **43G** | SALT **1.7G**

✱

Prep: 35 mins
Cook: 30 mins

Harissa Turkey Burgers

Serves 4

250g (9oz) pouch of cooked mixed grains (or 250g/9oz home-cooked mixed grains)
500g (1lb 2oz) lean minced turkey breast
2 large garlic cloves, finely grated
1 tsp coriander seeds, toasted and crushed
4 tbsp rose harissa
small bunch of parsley, finely chopped
2 red peppers
150g (5½oz) rocket
2 tbsp rapeseed oil
juice of 1 lemon
3 cooked beetroot, grated
4 wholemeal seeded buns, toasted, to serve

For the sauce

1 courgette
½ small bunch of dill, finely chopped
4 tbsp 0% Greek yogurt
2 tbsp low-fat mayonnaise

1. Tip the grains into a bowl and use your hands to mix in the minced turkey, garlic, coriander seeds, harissa and parsley. Shape into four patties. Cover and chill. You can freeze the patties at this stage – transfer to a freezerproof container, with a square of baking parchment in between each one, and put in the freezer for up to three months. Defrost in the fridge overnight before continuing.
2. To make the sauce, coarsely grate the courgette, discarding the seeds, then wrap in a clean cloth and squeeze out any liquid. Put in a bowl and mix with the dill, yogurt, 2 tbsp water and the mayonnaise.
3. Heat a grill to its highest setting and grill the peppers for 15–20 mins, turning halfway, until blistered and starting to char. Leave to cool a little, then peel and cut into strips, discarding the seeds. Toss the rocket with half the oil and the lemon juice.
4. Heat the remaining oil in a frying pan over a medium heat and fry the burger patties for 6 mins each side. Serve with the sauce, grilled peppers, grated beetroot, toasted buns and the rocket salad so that everyone can assemble their own burger.

NUTRITIONAL INFO

PER SERVING KCAL **500** | FAT **22G** | SATURATES **3G** | CARBS **27G** | SUGARS **10G** | FIBRE **9G** | PROTEIN **44G** | SALT **0.9G**

Fish

✱

Prep: 10 mins
Cook: 35 mins

Coconut & Kale Fish Curry

Serves 4

- 1 tbsp rapeseed oil
- 1 onion, sliced
- thumb-sized piece of ginger, peeled and sliced into matchsticks
- 1 tsp turmeric
- 3–4 tbsp mild curry paste (Keralan works well)
- 150g (5½oz) cherry tomatoes, halved
- 150g (5½oz) kale, chopped
- 1 red chilli, halved
- 325ml (11fl oz) reduced-fat coconut milk
- 300ml (10fl oz) low-salt stock
- 100g (3½oz) raw king prawns, peeled and de-veined
- 2 skinless cod fillets, cut into chunks
- 250g (9oz) brown rice
- juice of 2 limes
- ½ small bunch of coriander, chopped
- handful of toasted coconut flakes (optional)

1. Heat the oil in a flameproof casserole dish. Cook the onion with a pinch of salt for 10 mins until it starts to caramelize. Stir through the ginger, turmeric and curry paste and cook for 2 mins.
2. Add the tomatoes, kale and chilli, then pour in the coconut milk and stock. Simmer for 10–15 mins or until the tomatoes begin to soften. Scoop out the chilli and discard. If not eating immediately, you can now freeze the curry base. Let it cool completely, then divide the curry between freezerproof containers, add the raw prawns and cod on top and freeze for up to two months. Defrost thoroughly in the fridge overnight.
3. Cook the rice following pack instructions. Meanwhile, gently stir the prawns and cod through the hot curry base and cook for 3–5 mins until opaque. If cooking after defrosting, reheat in a pan for 10 mins until piping hot and the prawns and fish are cooked through.
4. To serve, squeeze over the lime juice and stir through half the coriander. Scatter over the remaining coriander and the coconut flakes, if you like. Serve with the rice.

NUTRITIONAL INFO

PER SERVING KCAL **465** | FAT **15G** | SATURATES **6G** | CARBS **52G** | SUGARS **7G** | FIBRE **6G** | PROTEIN **28G** | SALT **1.5G**

Prep: 15 mins
Cook: 15 mins

Mango, Lime & Chilli Prawn Fishcakes

Serves 4

400g (14oz) raw prawns, peeled and de-veined
60g (2¼oz) mango flesh, finely chopped, plus extra chunks to serve
zest of 1 lime
2 garlic cloves, crushed
10g (¼oz) ginger, grated, or 1 tsp ginger paste
small handful of coriander, finely chopped
1 egg, beaten
3 tbsp plain flour
½ red chilli (deseeded if you don't like it too hot), finely chopped (optional)
1 tbsp vegetable oil

To serve

cooked sticky rice or noodles
finely sliced carrot and cucumber
satay sauce

1 Tip the prawns into a food processor and blitz to a fine paste. Transfer to a large bowl and add the mango, lime zest, garlic, ginger, coriander, beaten egg, flour and chilli, if using. Season and mix well.

2 Heat the oil in a frying pan over a medium heat. Take a tablespoon of the mixture and, using the back of another spoon, push it into the frying pan in a circle like a pancake. Working in batches, fry the fishcakes for 8–10 mins until golden on each side and cooked through. You should end up with 12 fishcakes. If you want to save some for another day, let the cooked fishcakes cool completely before freezing them for up to two months. Defrost thoroughly in the fridge overnight, then reheat on a baking sheet in the oven at 200°C/180°C fan/400°F/Gas Mark 6 for 5 mins.

3 Serve over sticky rice or noodles, with sliced cucumber and carrot and mango chunks, alongside some satay sauce.

NUTRITIONAL INFO

PER SERVING KCAL **187** | FAT **5G** | SATURATES **1G** | CARBS **14G** | SUGARS **1G** | FIBRE **1G** | PROTEIN **21G** | SALT **0.6G**

*

Prep: 10 mins
Cook: 15 mins

Mediterranean Fish Stew

Serves 2

1 tbsp olive oil
½ fennel bulb, finely sliced
1 small onion, finely chopped
2 garlic cloves, crushed
250ml (9fl oz) vegetable stock
1 tsp smoked paprika
400g (14oz) can cherry tomatoes
1 tsp sherry vinegar
pinch of golden caster sugar
2 skinless hake fillets or any other white fish
small handful of parsley, finely chopped
crusty bread, to serve

1 Heat the oil in a deep, lidded frying pan over a high heat and fry the fennel, onion and garlic for 1 min. Pour in the stock and bring to a simmer, then cook for 5 mins until the veg are tender.

2 Stir in the paprika, tomatoes, vinegar and sugar. Simmer gently for 5 mins until thickened slightly. If not eating immediately, you can now freeze the stew. Leave it to cool completely, then transfer to a freezerproof container. Freeze the uncooked fish separately. Defrost both in the fridge overnight, then reheat the sauce for 5 mins until bubbling before continuing.

3 Nestle the fish into the mixture and cover. Cook for 5 mins more until the fish is tender and cooked through and the stew is piping hot. Check the seasoning, sprinkle over the parsley, then serve with crusty bread on the side.

NUTRITIONAL INFO

PER SERVING KCAL **253** | FAT **9G** | SATURATES **1G** | CARBS **14G** | SUGARS **13G** | FIBRE **6G** | PROTEIN **26G** | SALT **0.7G**

✳

Prep: 15 mins
Cook: 25 mins

Fish Tagine with Saffron & Almonds

Serves 4

1 tbsp olive oil
1 onion, chopped
good pinch of saffron threads
600ml (20fl oz) fish or chicken stock
2 garlic cloves, crushed
thumb-sized piece of ginger, peeled and grated
½ green chilli (deseeded if you don't like it too hot), finely sliced
2 tsp ground cumin
1 tsp ground coriander
1 tsp ground cinnamon
1 tbsp tomato purée
10 cherry tomatoes, halved
2 tbsp ground almonds
zest of 1 orange and juice of ½
1 tbsp honey
700g (1lb 9oz) skinless white fish fillets, cut into large chunks
small bunch of coriander, chopped
handful of flaked almonds, toasted

To serve

½ green chilli (deseeded if you don't like it too hot), finely sliced
cooked couscous (optional)
natural yogurt (optional)

1 Heat the oil in a large, lidded pan. Add the onion and cook for a few minutes until soft. Meanwhile, put the saffron in the hot stock and leave to steep.

2 Add the garlic, ginger and green chilli to the pan and cook for a few minutes more, before tipping in the spices and tomato purée. Stir for a few minutes until fragrant, then add the tomatoes, ground almonds, orange zest and juice, honey and saffron-scented stock, making sure you use all of the saffron threads. Simmer, uncovered, for 10 mins until the tomatoes have broken down and the sauce has thickened a little. If you don't plan to eat this immediately, leave the sauce to cool completely, then freeze it in a freezerproof container. Freeze the uncooked fish separately. Defrost both the sauce and the fish in the fridge overnight. Reheat the sauce until piping hot before continuing.

3 Add the fish to the pan, making sure the pieces are all nestled into the sauce. Cover with the lid and simmer over a low heat for 2–3 mins until just cooked. Check the seasoning, add the fresh coriander and scatter with the flaked almonds. Serve scattered with the green chilli, along with some couscous and a blob of natural yogurt, if you like.

NUTRITIONAL INFO

PER SERVING KCAL **299** | FAT **11G** | SATURATES **1G** | CARBS **10G** | SUGARS **9G** | FIBRE **2G** | PROTEIN **41G** | SALT **0.7G**

Easy Fish Pie

Prep: 15 mins
Cook: 45 mins

Serves 4–6

1kg (2lb 4oz) Maris Piper potatoes, peeled and halved
400ml (14fl oz) milk, plus a splash
25g (1oz) butter, plus an extra knob
25g (1oz) plain flour
4 spring onions, finely sliced
pack of fish pie mix (cod, salmon, smoked haddock etc.), about 325g–400g (11½–14oz)
1 tsp Dijon or English mustard
½ a 25g (1oz) pack of chives, finely snipped
handful of frozen sweetcorn
handful of frozen petits pois
handful of grated cheddar

1. Put the potatoes in a large saucepan and pour over enough water to cover them. Bring to the boil, then simmer until tender. Drain thoroughly and mash with a splash of milk and a knob of butter. Season with black pepper. If you're planning to freeze the fish pie for future use, let the mashed potato cool completely before continuing.
2. Put the remaining butter, flour and spring onions in another pan and heat gently until the butter has melted, stirring regularly. Cook for 1–2 mins. Gradually whisk in the remaining milk. Bring to the boil, stirring well to avoid any lumps in the sauce or sticking to the bottom of the pan. Cook for 3–4 mins until thickened. If you're planning to freeze the fish pie for future use, let the white sauce cool completely before continuing.
3. Off the heat, stir in the fish, mustard, chives, sweetcorn and petits pois. Spoon into an ovenproof dish. Spoon the potato on top and sprinkle with the grated cheese. You can now freeze your fish pie – cover and pop in the freezer for up to two months. Defrost thoroughly in the fridge overnight before continuing.
4. Heat the oven to 200°C/180°C fan/400°F/Gas mark 6. Pop the fish pie in the oven for 20–25 mins (25–30 mins if cooking, uncovered, from chilled) or until golden and bubbling at the edges.

NUTRITIONAL INFO

PER SERVING (IF SERVING 4) KCAL **430** | FAT **15.63G** | SATURATES **8G** | CARBS **50.13G** | SUGARS **7G** | FIBRE **5G** | PROTEIN **27.1G** | SALT **1.25G**

✱

Prep: 15 mins
Cook: 20 mins

Pesto Salmon & Bean Gratins

Serves 6

100g (3½oz) baby spinach

3 x 400g (14oz) cans cannellini beans, drained

300g (10½oz) cherry tomatoes, halved

2 tbsp olive oil

zest and juice of 1 lemon

6 tbsp soft cheese

4 tbsp pesto

150g (5½oz) dried breadcrumbs

40g (1½oz) parmesan, grated

3 tbsp pine nuts

6 salmon fillets, skin removed

crusty bread, to serve (optional)

1 Divide the spinach between six individual baking dishes (make sure the dishes are safe to use in both the freezer and the oven). Spoon over the beans and tomatoes and drizzle with the oil. Scatter over a little of the lemon zest and squeeze over some juice, then season well. Toss everything together with your hands, like you would a salad.

2 Mix the soft cheese and pesto together in one bowl, and the breadcrumbs, parmesan and pine nuts in another. Season the salmon fillets and lay one in each dish, then spread the soft cheese mixture over the fillets. Scatter with the cheesy breadcrumbs, pressing onto the salmon (it's okay if they also get on the veg and beans a little).

3 If you want to cook straight away, heat the oven to 200°C/180°C fan/400°F/Gas Mark 6 and bake for 20–25 mins or until the salmon is cooked through and the crumbs are golden. Alternatively, cover the dishes well and freeze for up to two months – it's a good idea to write the name of the dish and the cooking instructions on the lid. To cook from frozen, uncover and bake for 30–35 mins at 200°C/180°C fan/400°F/Gas Mark 6.

4 Serve the gratins with some crusty bread for mopping up the juices, if you like.

NUTRITIONAL INFO

PER SERVING KCAL **793** | FAT **44G** | SATURATES **12G** | CARBS **41G** | SUGARS **6G** | FIBRE **9G** | PROTEIN **53G** | SALT **1.6G**

Chunky Fish Fingers

Prep: 15 mins
Cook: 15 mins

Serves 2

100g (3½oz) plain flour, seasoned
3 large eggs, beaten
200g (7oz) dried breadcrumbs
large pinch of turmeric (optional)
500g (1lb 2oz) skinless chunky white fish fillets (we used haddock), cut into neat thumb-sized strips
vegetable oil, for frying

1 Tip the seasoned flour onto a plate, put the beaten egg in a bowl and tip the breadcrumbs into another bowl. If you want the breadcrumbs to be golden, mix through the turmeric. Place a large empty plate at the end of the line to put the uncooked fish fingers on.

2 To assemble your chunky fish fingers, dip each fish strip in the flour, then into the egg (shaking off any excess) and finally toss in the breadcrumbs. Using just one hand for the breadcrumbs is less messy. Transfer the coated fish fingers to a baking tray. If keeping for a later date, open-freeze the fish fingers and, when they are solid, transfer them to a freezerproof container.

3 Heat a little oil in a frying pan and cook them for 2–3 mins on each side (3–4 mins if cooking from frozen). Put on a baking tray lined with baking parchment and keep warm in a low oven, if cooking in batches. Alternatively, if cooking from frozen, preheat the oven to 200°C/180°C fan/400°F/Gas Mark 6. Brush a baking tray with a little oil, add the frozen fish fingers and cook for 10–12 mins until golden and cooked through, turning them halfway through the cooking time.

NUTRITIONAL INFO

PER SERVING KCAL **399** | FAT **12G** | SATURATES **2G** | CARBS **43.3G** | SUGARS **1.3G** | FIBRE **2G** | PROTEIN **29.3G** | SALT **1.1G**

Spicy Fish Stew

✱

Prep: 10 mins
Cook: 40 mins

Serves 4

- 1 tbsp olive oil
- 2 onions, thinly sliced
- 3 spring onions, chopped
- 3 garlic cloves, chopped
- 1 red chilli, deseeded and thinly sliced
- a few thyme sprigs
- 2 x 400g (14oz) cans chopped tomatoes
- 400ml (14fl oz) vegetable bouillon made with 2 tsp vegetable bouillon powder
- 2 green peppers, cut into pieces
- 160g (5¾oz) brown basmati rice
- 400g (14oz) can plus 210g (7½oz) can red kidney beans, drained
- handful of coriander, chopped, plus a few extra sprigs to serve
- handful of flat-leaf parsley, chopped
- zest of 1 lime
- 550g (1lb 4oz) salmon, skin removed and cut into large pieces

1. Heat the oil in a large, lidded nonstick pan. Add the onions and cook for 8–10 mins until softened and golden. Add the spring onions, garlic, chilli and thyme and cook, stirring, for 1 min. Pour in the tomatoes and bouillon, then stir in the peppers. Cover and leave to simmer for 15 mins.
2. Stir the beans in with the sauce, along with the coriander and parsley, and leave to cook gently for another 10 mins until the peppers are tender. Add the lime zest. If freezing for another day, leave the stew to cool completely at this stage, then divide between freezerproof containers and pop in the freezer, freezing the uncooked salmon separately. Defrost both in the fridge overnight. Reheat the stew for 5 mins until bubbling before continuing.
3. Meanwhile, cook the rice according to pack instructions.
4. Add the salmon to the stew, stir, cover the pan and cook for 4–5 mins until cooked through and the salmon is piping hot. Ladle into bowls and scatter with the extra coriander sprigs.

NUTRITIONAL INFO

PER SERVING KCAL **664** | FAT **26G** | SATURATES **5G** | CARBS **58G** | SUGARS **14G** | FIBRE **14G** | PROTEIN **42G** | SALT **0.3G**

Veg

V

Prep: 5 mins
Cook: 20 mins

Spicy Cauliflower & Halloumi Rice

Serves 4

- 1 small head of cauliflower (about 500g/1lb 2oz), broken into medium florets
- 150g (5½oz) baby spinach
- 1 tbsp rapeseed oil
- 1 red onion, sliced
- 120g (4¼oz) halloumi, cut into cubes
- 1 garlic clove, crushed
- thumb-sized piece of ginger, finely grated
- 1 tsp turmeric
- 1 tbsp medium curry powder
- 2 x 250g (9oz) pouches of ready-to-eat brown basmati rice
- 1 red chilli, finely sliced

1 Bring a large pan of salted water to the boil and cook the cauliflower for 5 mins over a high heat, adding the spinach for the final 2 mins. Drain and set aside.

2 Heat the oil in a shallow, flameproof casserole dish or large frying pan and fry the onion over a medium heat for 5 mins. Turn up the heat, add the halloumi and cook for a further 5 mins, then add the garlic, ginger, turmeric and curry powder and cook for 1 min more. Stir through the rice, cauliflower and spinach and warm everything through, adding 1 tbsp water if it looks a little dry. Season and scatter over the chilli before serving.

3 You can make this dish in advance and chill until needed or keep any leftovers in the fridge for another day – it will last well for up to three days. Reheat to serve, adding a little more water if needed.

NUTRITIONAL INFO

PER SERVING KCAL **337** | FAT **14G** | SATURATES **6G** | CARBS **36G** | SUGARS **5G** | FIBRE **7G** | PROTEIN **14G** | SALT **1.01G**

✳ V Ve

Vegan Bolognese

Prep: 20 mins
Cook: 1 hr

Serves 3

15g (½oz) dried porcini mushrooms
1½ tbsp olive oil
½ onion, finely chopped
1 carrot, finely chopped
1 celery stick, finely chopped
2 garlic cloves, sliced
2 thyme sprigs
½ tsp tomato purée
50ml (2fl oz) vegan red wine (optional)
125g (4½oz) dried green lentils
400g (14oz) can whole plum tomatoes
125g (4½oz) chestnut mushrooms, chopped
125g (4½oz) Portobello mushrooms, sliced
½ tsp soy sauce
½ tsp yeast extract, such as Marmite
270g (9½oz) dried spaghetti
handful of basil leaves

1 Pour 400ml (14fl oz) boiling water over the dried porcini and leave for 10 mins until rehydrated. Meanwhile, pour 1 tbsp of the oil into a large, lidded saucepan. Add the onion, carrot, celery and a pinch of salt. Cook gently, stirring, for 10 mins until soft. Remove the porcini from the liquid, keeping the mushroom stock, and roughly chop. Set both aside.

2 Add the garlic and thyme to the pan. Cook for 1 min, then stir in the tomato purée and cook for 1 min more. Pour in the red wine, if using, and cook until nearly reduced, then add the lentils, reserved mushroom stock and tomatoes. Bring to the boil, then reduce the heat, cover and leave to simmer.

3 Meanwhile, heat a large frying pan. Add the remaining oil, then tip in the chestnut, Portobello and rehydrated porcini mushrooms. Fry until all the water has evaporated and the mushrooms are a deep golden brown. Pour in the soy sauce. Give everything a good mix, then scrape the mushrooms into the lentil mixture.

4 Stir in the yeast extract and continue to cook the ragu, stirring occasionally, over a low–medium heat for 30–45 mins until the lentils are cooked and the sauce is thick and reduced. Add a little extra water if necessary. Remove the thyme sprigs and season to taste. If not eating immediately, let the ragu cool completely. It can then be frozen for up to two months. Defrost thoroughly in the fridge overnight and reheat in a pan until piping hot.

5 Cook the spaghetti in a large pan of salted water for 1 min less than pack instructions. Drain the pasta, reserving a ladleful of pasta water, then toss the spaghetti in the sauce. Use a little of the starchy liquid to loosen up the ragu slightly so that the pasta clings to the sauce. Serve topped with the basil and some black pepper.

NUTRITIONAL INFO

PER SERVING KCAL **599** | FAT **8G** | SATURATES **1G** | CARBS **97G** | SUGARS **12G** | FIBRE **13G** | PROTEIN **25G** | SALT **0.3G**

✻ V Ve

Easy Vegetarian Chilli

Prep: 25 mins
Cook: 55 mins

Serves 8

2 tbsp vegetable oil
2 carrots, finely chopped
2 celery sticks, finely chopped
2 onions, finely chopped
2 tsp dried mixed herbs
2 garlic cloves, crushed or finely grated
1 red pepper, sliced
1 green pepper, sliced
2–3 tsp chilli powder (depending on how hot you like it)
2 tsp sweet smoked paprika
2 tbsp tomato purée
400g (14oz) can red kidney beans, drained
400g (14oz) can black beans, drained
2 x 400g (14oz) cans chopped tomatoes
400ml (14fl oz) vegetable stock

To serve

chopped coriander
cooked rice
grated cheddar
soured cream (or dairy-free alternative), optional

1 Heat the oil in a large saucepan over a low–medium heat and fry the carrots, celery, onions and mixed herbs for 10–12 mins, stirring occasionally, until the veg are soft but not golden. You may need to add a splash of water if the veg start to catch.

2 Stir in the garlic and both the peppers and cook for a further 5 mins until the peppers begin to soften. Sprinkle in the chilli powder and paprika and turn up the heat to medium, then stir and cook for 1 min. Mix in the tomato purée and cook for a further 1 min, then tip in all of the beans, the tomatoes and the stock.

3 Stir well and bring to the boil, then reduce the heat to a simmer. Cook for 25–35 mins until the beans are cooked and the sauce has thickened. If not eating immediately, or if you have leftovers, let the chilli cool completely. It can then be frozen for up to two months. Defrost thoroughly in the fridge overnight and reheat in a pan until piping hot.

4 Serve scattered with chopped coriander along with rice, grated cheddar and soured cream, if you like.

NUTRITIONAL INFO

PER SERVING KCAL **157** | FAT **4G** | SATURATES **0.3G** | CARBS **19G** | SUGARS **10G** | FIBRE **9G** | PROTEIN **7G** | SALT **0.25G**

✳ V

Prep: 1 hr and 15 mins
Cook: 45 mins

Smoky Aubergine, Mozzarella & Harissa Lasagne

Serves 8

6 aubergines
2 tbsp olive oil
1 onion, finely chopped
2 large garlic cloves, crushed
4 tbsp rose harissa
3 tsp coriander seeds, crushed
400g (14oz) can chopped tomatoes
2 tbsp tomato purée
1 tsp golden caster sugar
1 tsp red wine vinegar or balsamic vinegar
1 tsp dried mint
½ small bunch of flat-leaf parsley, finely chopped
300g (10½oz) dried lasagne sheets
3 x 120g (4¼oz) balls of mozzarella, drained and grated

For the béchamel

750ml (1⅓ pints) whole milk
100g (3½oz) unsalted butter
75g (2¾oz) plain flour
200g (7oz) mature cheddar, grated

1 Working with the aubergines one at a time, carefully hold over the lit ring of a gas hob using tongs, turning until deeply charred all over. Alternatively, heat the grill to its highest setting and char the aubergines on a baking tray for about 15 mins, turning occasionally until completely blackened. Transfer the aubergines to a plate and leave to cool. When cool enough to handle, peel off the charred skin and remove the stems. Roughly chop the flesh into chunks and set aside.

2 Heat the oil in a large pan over a low heat and cook the onion with a pinch of salt for 10–15 mins until softened and translucent. Add the garlic and cook for 3 mins more, then add the harissa, coriander seeds, tomatoes and tomato purée. Bring to a simmer and stir in the sugar, vinegar and aubergine chunks. Season the ragu and cook, uncovered, for 10 mins, stirring often. Add the mint and parsley, then remove from the heat and set aside.

3 For the béchamel, warm the milk in a pan over a low heat until steaming. Melt the butter in a large saucepan, then stir through the flour and cook for 3 mins. Remove from the heat and slowly add the warm milk, whisking constantly. Return to a low heat, bring to a simmer and whisk constantly until thickened. Add 120g (4¼oz) of the cheddar and some salt to taste. Stir to melt the cheese.

4 Spread a spoonful each of the béchamel and ragu into the base of a deep baking dish (about 20 x 30cm/8 x 12 inches). Arrange a layer of lasagne sheets on top, followed by both sauces again and a layer of grated mozzarella. Repeat until you've used all the lasagne sheets and ragu, finishing with a final layer of béchamel, mozzarella and the remaining cheddar. If not eating the lasagne immediately, leave to cool completely, wrap it well and freeze for up to one month. Defrost at room temperature before continuing.

5 Heat the oven to 200°C/180°C fan/400°F/Gas Mark 6. Cook the lasagne for 40–45 mins, then allow to cool for 10 mins before serving.

NUTRITIONAL INFO

PER SERVING KCAL **649** | FAT **37G** | SATURATES **21G** | CARBS **48G** | SUGARS **14G** | FIBRE **10G** | PROTEIN **26G** | SALT **1.14G**

✱ V Ve

Easy Lentil Curry

Prep: 5 mins
Cook: 45 mins

Serves 4

2 tbsp sunflower oil
2 onions, cut into rough wedges
4 tbsp curry paste
850ml (1½ pints) vegetable stock
750g (1lb 10 oz) pack of frozen vegetables
100g (3½oz) dried red lentils
200g (7oz) basmati rice
1 tsp turmeric
handful of raisins
handful of roughly chopped flat-leaf parsley

To serve

poppadums
mango chutney

1. Heat the oil in a large, lidded pan. Add the onions and cook over a high heat for about 8 minutes or until they are golden brown. Stir in the curry paste and cook for 1 min. Slowly pour in a little of the stock so that it sizzles, scraping any bits from the bottom of the pan. Gradually pour in the rest of the stock.
2. Stir in the frozen vegetables, cover and simmer for 5 mins. Add the lentils and simmer for a further 15–20 mins or until the vegetables and lentils are cooked. If not eating immediately, let the curry cool completely. It can then be frozen for up to two months. Defrost thoroughly in the fridge overnight and reheat in a pan until piping hot.
3. While the curry is simmering, cook the rice following pack instructions, adding the turmeric to the cooking water. Drain well.
4. Season the curry with salt and toss in the raisins and chopped parsley, then serve with the rice and some poppadums and mango chutney.

NUTRITIONAL INFO

PER SERVING KCAL **498** | FAT **11G** | SATURATES **1G** | CARBS **78G** | SUGARS **18G** | FIBRE **6G** | PROTEIN **19G** | SALT **1.21G**

✳ V

Prep: 10 mins
Cook: 20 mins

Paneer, Chickpea & Spinach Curry

Serves 4

2 tbsp vegetable oil
1 onion, finely chopped
10g (¼oz) ginger, peeled and grated, or 1 tsp ginger paste
2 garlic cloves, crushed
1 tbsp medium curry powder
1 tsp garam masala
1 tsp turmeric
1 red chilli (deseeded if you don't like it too hot), finely chopped
200g (7oz) paneer, cut into 1cm (½ inch) cubes
2 x 400g (14oz) cans chickpeas, drained
400ml (14fl oz) can coconut milk
400g (14oz) frozen spinach
120ml (4fl oz) vegetable stock, made with 1 stock cube
1 tbsp mango chutney
juice of ½ lemon

To serve

steamed basmati rice
handful of coriander, chopped or leaves left whole
sliced chilli (optional)

1 Heat the oil in a deep frying pan over a medium heat. Add the onion and cook for 3–4 mins until soft. Stir through the ginger and garlic along with all the spices and chilli. Cook for 1–2 mins until fragrant.

2 Stir in the paneer and chickpeas. Add the coconut milk, spinach and stock. Bring to the boil, then reduce to a simmer and cook for 20 mins until reduced and thickened. If not eating immediately, let the curry cool completely. It can then be frozen for up to two months. Defrost thoroughly in the fridge overnight and reheat in a pan over a low–medium heat until piping hot.

3 Stir the mango chutney through, then season to taste and add the lemon juice. Serve with rice, fresh coriander on top and some sliced chilli, if you like.

NUTRITIONAL INFO

PER SERVING KCAL **604** | FAT **40G** | SATURATES **23G** | CARBS **29G** | SUGARS **7G** | FIBRE **11G** | PROTEIN **27G** | SALT **1G**

✱ V

Prep: 10 mins
Cook: 55 mins

Cheat's Beetroot Biryani

Serves 4

- 3 large (about 500g/1lb 2oz), raw beetroot, peeled and cut into 2cm (¾ inch) cubes
- 2 tbsp rapeseed oil
- 1 large onion, finely sliced
- thumb-sized piece of ginger, peeled and grated
- 2 small garlic cloves, crushed
- 1 bay leaf
- 4 cardamom pods
- 2 tsp turmeric
- 2 tbsp garam masala
- 250g (9oz) basmati rice, rinsed
- 500ml (18fl oz) low-salt vegetable stock
- 100ml (3½fl oz) fat-free natural yogurt
- small bunch of coriander
- your favourite chutney or pickle, to serve (optional)

1. Heat the oven to 200°C/180°C fan/400°F/Gas Mark 6. Toss the beetroot with half the oil and some seasoning, then tip into a roasting dish and cook for 25–30 mins, tossing halfway through, until tender.
2. Meanwhile, heat the remaining oil in a large, shallow, flameproof casserole dish or ovenproof frying pan. Fry the onion over a medium heat for 10 mins until golden. Add the ginger and half the garlic and cook for 1 min. Add the bay leaf, cardamom pods, turmeric and garam masala, stir, then cook for 2 mins. Stir in the rice and beetroot cubes, then season. Pour in the stock and bring to the boil.
3. Put in the oven, uncovered, and cook for 20–25 mins until the rice is cooked through. Give it a stir when it's out of the oven. If not eating immediately, or if you have leftovers, let the biryani cool completely. It can then be frozen for up to two months. Defrost thoroughly in the fridge overnight and reheat in a pan over a medium heat for 10–15 mins or until piping hot.
4. Put the yogurt, coriander and remaining garlic in a food processor and whizz until smooth. Season to taste. Serve the biriyani with the coriander yogurt and your favourite chutney or pickle, if you like.

NUTRITIONAL INFO

PER SERVING KCAL **366** | FAT **8G** | SATURATES **1G** | CARBS **66G** | SUGARS **12G** | FIBRE **5G** | PROTEIN **11G** | SALT **1.05G**

✱ V

Prep: 5 mins
Cook: 20 mins

Creamy Halloumi & Tomato Curry

Serves 2–3

- 2 tbsp neutral oil (such as vegetable or sunflower oil)
- 1 large onion, chopped
- 2 garlic cloves, crushed
- thumb-sized piece of ginger, peeled and grated
- 2 tsp ground cumin
- 2 tsp ground coriander
- 1 tsp turmeric
- 400g (14oz) can chopped tomatoes
- 100ml (3½fl oz) double cream, plus a little extra if needed
- 225g (8oz) block of halloumi, cut into bite-size cubes
- 80g (2¾oz) baby spinach, fresh or frozen
- 2 tsp golden caster sugar
- 1 tbsp garam masala
- 1 tsp nigella seeds
- cooked rice, grains or naan, to serve

1 Heat 1 tbsp of the oil in a large pan over a medium heat. Add the onion and cook for about 5 mins or until it turns translucent. Add the garlic and ginger to the pan. Cook for another 2 mins, stirring frequently, until they become fragrant. Stir in the cumin, coriander and turmeric and cook for 2 mins more. Pour in the tomatoes and stir well. Simmer for 5–7 mins or until the mixture thickens. Reduce the heat and add the cream. Stir and simmer gently for 3–4 mins until thickened.

2 While the sauce is simmering, heat the remaining oil in a separate pan over a medium–high heat. Fry the halloumi for 3–4 mins until golden brown on all sides.

3 Once the halloumi is browned, add it to the sauce along with the spinach, sugar and garam masala and stir to combine. Gently simmer for 5 mins until the spinach has wilted or defrosted. If the curry seems too thick, add a splash of water or more cream to loosen it. If not eating immediately, you can now leave the curry to cool completely and pop it in the freezer for up to two months. Defrost in the fridge overnight, then reheat gently until piping hot.

4 Scatter with the nigella seeds and serve with rice, grains or naan.

NUTRITIONAL INFO

PER SERVING (IF SERVING 3) KCAL **575** | FAT **45G** | SATURATES **24G** | CARBS **18G** | SUGARS **14G** | FIBRE **5G** | PROTEIN **23G** | SALT **2.3G**

V

Paneer Korma

Prep: 5 mins
Cook: 25 mins

Serves 4

3 tbsp vegetable oil
225g (8oz) block of paneer, cut into 2cm (¾ inch) cubes
1 large onion, roughly chopped
thumb-sized piece of ginger, peeled
2 large garlic cloves
5 tbsp korma paste
3 cardamom pods, crushed
70g (2½oz) ground almonds
500ml (18fl oz) vegetable stock
150g (5½oz) spinach
100ml (3½fl oz) Greek yogurt
cooked rice or naan, to serve (optional)

1 Heat 1 tbsp of the oil in a deep frying pan over a medium–high heat. Add the paneer cubes and fry for 5 mins, turning regularly, so that each side is golden brown. Remove with tongs, put on a plate lined with kitchen paper and set aside.

2 Put the onion, ginger and garlic in a food processor with a splash of water and blitz until completely smooth. Heat the remaining oil in the frying pan over a medium–low heat. Add the onion mixture and a pinch of salt and fry for 10 mins or until lightly golden. Add the korma paste and cardamom and fry for 1 min. Stir in the ground almonds and fry for 1 min to make a thick paste.

3 Add the stock, bring to a simmer and cook for 5–10 mins, uncovered, or until reduced a little. Add the spinach to the sauce and cook for 5 mins. Stir through the yogurt and paneer and season generously. Serve with rice or warm naan, if you like.

4 You can make this dish in advance and chill until needed or keep any leftovers in the fridge to be eaten another day – it will last well for up to three days.

NUTRITIONAL INFO

PER SERVING KCAL **509** | FAT **29G** | SATURATES **12G** | CARBS **21G** | SUGARS **12G** | FIBRE **16G** | PROTEIN **33G** | SALT **0.7G**

V

Prep: 30 mins
Cook: 1 hr

Caramelized Onion, Goat's Cheese & Za'atar Galette

Serves 6–8

3 tbsp olive oil
4 medium-large white onions, halved and thinly sliced
2 tbsp cider vinegar
2 tbsp light brown soft sugar
pinch of chilli flakes
1 tbsp za'atar
120g (4¼oz) soft goat's cheese
4 thyme sprigs, leaves picked

For the pastry

300g (10½oz) plain flour, plus extra for dusting
150g (5½oz) cold butter, cut into small pieces
1 egg, plus 1 egg yolk, beaten, to glaze
1 tbsp za'atar

1 Start by making the pastry. Tip the flour into a large bowl and add the butter and a good pinch of salt. Use your fingertips to rub the butter into the flour until it resembles fine breadcrumbs. Add the whole egg and 1 tbsp cold water and whisk together with a fork, then work the egg into the buttery flour crumbs until the pastry comes together, adding a splash more water if it seems dry. Don't overwork the pastry otherwise it will become tough. Shape the pastry into a disc and wrap in baking parchment, then chill until you're ready to use it.

2 Now make the filling. Heat the oil in a large frying pan over a low–medium heat and add the onions and a pinch of salt. Cook slowly for 10–15 mins, stirring now and then, until the onions are soft. Add the vinegar, sugar and chilli flakes and cook for another 5–10 mins until the onions are sticky and caramelized. Stir in the za'atar. Remove from the heat and leave to cool.

3 Remove the pastry from the fridge. If it is very firm, leave it at room temperature for 30 mins to make rolling easier. Heat the oven to 200°C/180°C fan/400°F/Gas Mark 6 with a baking sheet on the middle shelf to warm up. Place a large piece of baking parchment (roughly the size of the baking sheet) on your work surface and dust with a little flour. Roll out the pastry on the parchment to a circle roughly 33cm (13 inches) in diameter and about 3mm (⅛ inch) thick.

4 Spread the caramelized onions over the centre of the pastry, leaving a 1cm (½ inch) border around the edge. Break off small chunks of goat's cheese and scatter over the onions, then spinkle over the thyme leaves.

5 Fold the pastry edge inwards to create a border around the tart, leaving the filling exposed. Brush the pastry with the egg yolk and sprinkle the za'atar on the crust. Remove the tray from the oven and slide the sheet of parchment and tart on top. Bake for 40 mins until golden brown. Leave to cool for 5–10 mins before serving. The galette will keep in the fridge for up to four days. To reheat leftovers, warm them through in a low oven (120°C/100°C fan/250°F/Gas Mark ½).

NUTRITIONAL INFO

PER SERVING (IF SERVING 8) KCAL **455** | FAT **26G** | SATURATES **14G** | CARBS **43G** | SUGARS **12G** | FIBRE **5G** | PROTEIN **10G** | SALT **0.63G**

✱ V Ve

Next-Level Ratatouille

Prep: 20 mins
Cook: 2 hrs

Serves 6

3 red peppers, quartered
handful of basil, stalks and leaves separated
large thyme sprig
2 tbsp olive oil, plus extra for frying and drizzling as required
2 courgettes (different colours are good), roughly chopped
1 aubergine, chopped into large chunks
1 red onion, roughly chopped
4 garlic cloves, sliced
pinch of golden caster sugar
1 tbsp red wine vinegar
2 x 400g (14oz) cans cherry tomatoes
1 tbsp extra virgin olive oil
griddled sourdough, to serve

1. Heat the grill to high. Lay the pepper quarters, skin-side up, on a baking tray and grill until the skins are black and charred. Tip into a bowl, cover and leave to cool. When cool, peel the charred skin off the peppers, then cut the peppers into strips and toss back in the juices collected in the bowl. Tie the basil stalks and the thyme sprig together using kitchen string and set aside.
2. Heat the oven to 160°C/140°C fan/325°F/Gas Mark 3. Heat the olive oil in a lidded, flameproof casserole dish and fry the courgettes and aubergine for 15 mins until nicely browned. You may need to do this in batches, adding more oil to the pan as needed.
3. Scoop the veg out of the pan and set aside. Add a drizzle more oil, tip in the onion and cook for 15 mins until softened and starting to brown. Add the garlic and leave to sizzle for 1 min. Scatter with the sugar and leave for 1 min to caramelize, then splash in the vinegar. Stir in all the cooked vegetables, including the pepper juice, season generously, pour over the tomatoes and bring everything to a simmer.
4. Nestle in the herb bunch, cover the dish and transfer to the oven for 1 hr. Remove the lid and give it another 30 mins until everything is cooked down and jammy. If not eating immediately, or if you have leftovers, let the ratatouille cool completely. It can then be frozen for up to two months. Defrost thoroughly in the fridge overnight, then reheat and continue.
5. Leave the ratatouille to cool until just warm, then stir through most of the basil leaves and the extra virgin olive oil. Scatter with the remaining basil leaves and serve with griddled sourdough.

NUTRITIONAL INFO

PER SERVING KCAL **185** | FAT **12G** | SATURATES **2G** | CARBS **13G** | SUGARS **12G** | FIBRE **6G** | PROTEIN **4G** | SALT **0.03G**

✱ V

Prep: 5 mins
Cook: 20 mins

Enchilada Pie

Serves 2

1 tbsp vegetable or rapeseed oil
2 peppers, any colour you like, sliced
1 red onion, halved and sliced
400g (14oz) can mixed beans, drained
2 tsp–2 tbsp fajita spice mix (depending on how spicy you like it)
400g (14oz) can chopped tomatoes
small handful of coriander, chopped
4 corn tortillas
100ml (3½fl oz) soured cream
30g (1oz) cheddar, grated

1 Heat the oil in a pan. Fry the peppers and onion for about 10 mins until soft. Add the beans, fajita spice mix, tomatoes and some seasoning. Bubble for 5 mins to reduce the tomatoes a little, then stir in most of the coriander. Warm the tortillas in the microwave for 30 seconds.

2 Spread a quarter of the pepper and onion mixture over the base of an ovenproof dish (a round one, if possible) or frying pan. Top with some of the soured cream and a warm tortilla, then repeat the layers three more times, finishing off with a final layer of soured cream. Sprinkle over the cheese and leave to cool. You can now freeze the pie for up to two months. Defrost thoroughly in the fridge overnight before continuing.

3 Heat the grill to high. Put the pie under the grill for 5–7 mins or until golden and bubbling. Scatter with the remaining coriander before serving.

NUTRITIONAL INFO

PER SERVING KCAL **569** | FAT **26G** | SATURATES **12G** | CARBS **55G** | SUGARS **22G** | FIBRE **18G** | PROTEIN **19G** | SALT **1G**

✳ V

Prep: 50 mins
Cook: 1 hr and 5 mins

Cheesy Potato Patchwork Pie

Serves 6

500g (1lb 2oz) Maris Piper potatoes, unpeeled and cut into 1 cm (½ inch) thick slices
1 tbsp neutral oil (such as rapeseed or sunflower)
1 tbsp butter, plus extra for the dish
500g leeks (1lb 2oz), halved lengthways and sliced
2 garlic cloves, finely sliced
5 thyme sprigs
2 bay leaves
1 tbsp plain flour
½ tsp ground mace or a pinch of ground nutmeg
1 tbsp Dijon mustard
300ml (10fl oz) milk
50g (1¾oz) parmesan (or vegetarian alternative), grated
100g (3½oz) extra-mature cheddar, grated
steamed greens or watercress salad, to serve (optional)

For the pastry

250g (9oz) plain flour, plus extra for dusting
125g (4½oz) salted butter, cold and cut into small pieces
1 egg, plus 1 egg yolk
1 tbsp milk
5 thyme sprigs, leaves picked

1 To make the pastry, tip the flour and butter into a large bowl along with ½ tsp finely ground black pepper. Use your fingertips to rub the butter into the flour until it resembles fine breadcrumbs. In a jug, whisk together the whole egg, egg yolk, milk and thyme leaves with a fork. Pour three-quarters of the egg mixture into the buttery flour crumbs and stir it in using a cutlery knife. Use your hands to bring the pastry together into a smooth disc, wrap in baking parchment and chill for 30 mins.

2 Tip the potatoes into a lidded saucepan, cover with cold water and add a generous sprinkling of salt. Cover with the lid and bring to the boil, then reduce to a simmer and cook for 7–9 mins until almost tender – a sharp knife should slide in easily. Drain well and set aside to steam-dry.

3 Heat the oil and butter in a frying pan over a medium heat. Stir in the leeks, garlic, thyme sprigs and bay leaves with a pinch of salt and pepper. Cook for 20–22 mins until softened. Mix in the flour and mace or nutmeg and cook for a couple of minutes before stirring in the mustard. Remove from the heat and season to taste.

4 Slowly pour the milk in, stirring well, then mix in the parmesan and cheddar. Warm over a low heat until the cheese has melted. Remove the bay leaves and thyme sprigs. Butter a 25cm (10 inch) round ovenproof dish and arrange the potatoes on the bottom. Pour over the leek mixture and set aside to cool to room temperature.

5 Lightly dust a clean work surface with flour and roll out the pastry to around 5mm (¼ inch) thick – you don't need to be too precise. Cut into small rectangles, around 3 x 6cm (1¼ x 2½ inches), and arrange these over the top of the pie haphazardly, making sure they mostly overlap, leaving some steam holes, until the pie is completely covered. You can now freeze the pie, uncooked, for up to two months. Defrost in the fridge overnight before continuing.

6 Heat the oven to 220°C/200°C fan/425°F/Gas Mark 7. Brush the remaining egg mixture over the top of the pie and cook for 30–35 mins. Remove from the oven and leave to rest for 10 mins before serving.

NUTRITIONAL INFO

PER SERVING KCAL **604** | FAT **34G** | SATURATES **19G** | CARBS **53G** | SUGARS **5G** | FIBRE **6G** | PROTEIN **18G** | SALT **1.2G**

Sides & Salads

✳ V Ve

Prep: 10 mins
Cook: 10 mins

Wholemeal Flatbreads

Makes 8

350g (12oz) wholemeal flour, plus extra for dusting

4 tsp cold-pressed rapeseed oil

1 Put the flour in a medium bowl and rub in the oil with your fingertips. Stir in 225ml (8fl oz) warm water and mix thoroughly, then knead in the bowl until the dough feels smooth and elastic.

2 Put the dough onto a lightly floured work surface and divide into eight balls. Sprinkle the work surface with a little more flour and roll out one of the balls very thinly, using a floured rolling pin, to around 22cm (8½ inches) in diameter. Turn the dough regularly and sprinkle with a little more flour if it begins to stick. Set aside, then make the other flatbreads in the same way. If you're not eating immediately, you can now freeze them in a stack with baking parchment between each one for up to three months. Defrost thoroughly at room temperature before cooking as below.

3 Place a medium nonstick frying pan over a high heat. Once hot, add one of the flatbreads and cook for about 30 seconds, then turn over and cook on the other side for 30 seconds. Press the flatbread with a spatula while cooking to encourage it to puff up and cook inside – it should be lightly browned in patches and look fairly dry, without being crisp. Repeat with the remaining flatbreads, keeping them warm by wrapping in a clean tea towel until needed.

NUTRITIONAL INFO

PER FLATBREAD KCAL **168** | FAT **2G** | SATURATES **0G** | CARBS **27G** | SUGARS **1G** | FIBRE **5G** | PROTEIN **6G** | SALT **0G**

✱ V

Naan

Prep: 20 mins
Cook: 35 mins

Serves 6–8

- 7g (¼oz) sachet of fast-action dried yeast
- 2 tsp golden caster sugar
- 300g (10½oz) strong white bread flour, plus extra for dusting
- ½ tsp baking powder
- 25g (1oz) butter or ghee, melted, plus an extra 2–3 tbsp for the bowl and for brushing
- 150ml (5fl oz) natural yogurt
- 1 tbsp nigella seeds

1. Put 125ml (4fl oz) warm water into a bowl and sprinkle over the yeast and 1 tsp of the sugar. Leave for 10–15 mins or until frothy.
2. In a larger bowl, put the flour, remaining sugar, the baking powder and ½ tsp salt. Mix together, then make a well in the centre and add the melted butter or ghee, yogurt, nigella seeds and yeast mixture. Stir well, then start to bring the mixture together with your hands. If it's very wet, add a spoonful of flour; if it's dry, add a splash more warm water. It should be a soft dough but not so wet that it won't come together into a ball.
3. When you're happy with the consistency, start kneading the dough in the bowl, then transfer onto a well-floured work surface and continue to knead for 10 mins or until smooth and elastic but still soft. Butter a large bowl, then shape the dough into a ball and place in the bowl. Cover and leave in a warm place for 1 hr or until doubled in size.
4. Divide the dough into six balls and put them on a baking tray dusted with flour, then cover the tray with a damp tea towel. Heat a large nonstick frying pan over a high heat. Working with one ball of dough at a time, roll it out to form a teardrop shape approximately 21cm (8¼ inches) long and around 13cm (5 inches) at the widest part. When the pan is very hot, carefully lay the naan into it. Let it dry-fry and puff up for about 3 mins, then turn over and cook on the other side for another 3–4 mins or until cooked through and charred in patches.
5. Heat the oven to its lowest setting and put the cooked naan on a baking sheet. Brush with a little melted butter or ghee and cover with foil. Keep warm in the oven and layer up the cooked naans one on top of each other as you make them, brushing each one with melted butter or ghee as you go. Serve warm with curry or dips.
6. If you're making them in advance, allow them to cool, then stack them in a freezerproof container, with a layer of baking parchment between each one, and pop them in the freezer for up to two months. Defrost thoroughly at room temperature, then warm through in a low oven (160°C/140°C fan/325°F/Gas Mark 3) for 5–10 mins until hot.

NUTRITIONAL INFO

PER SERVING (IF SERVING 8) KCAL **224** | FAT **8G** | SATURATES **4G** | CARBS **31G** | SUGARS **3G** | FIBRE **1G** | PROTEIN **6G** | SALT **0.57G**

✱ V Ve

Prep: 20 mins
Cook: 1 hr and 50 mins

Triple-Cooked Roast Potatoes

Serves 6

250g (9oz) beef dripping, goose fat or vegetable oil

1.5kg (3lb 5oz) Maris Piper or King Edward potatoes

2 tbsp semolina or plain flour

1. Heat the oven to 220°C/200°C fan/425°F/Gas Mark 7. Tip the dripping, fat or oil into a deep roasting tin and put in the oven to heat up. Peel the potatoes and cut into roughly 5cm (2 inch) chunks. Or, for larger potatoes, quarter them. Cook in a large, lidded pan of salted boiling water for 6–8 mins until the outside of the potatoes are starting to soften. Drain well, then leave to steam-dry for a few minutes.
2. Return the potatoes to the pan. Sprinkle over the semolina or flour, cover with the lid and shake well to fluff the potatoes up.
3. Remove the roasting tin from the oven and carefully tip in the potatoes. Baste in the hot fat or oil so that they're fully coated. Roast in a single layer for 20 mins, then remove from the oven, turn and baste again. Roast for a further 20 mins, then repeat and roast for a final 10–20 mins until golden and crisp. If you're not eating immediately, transfer to a plate using a slotted spoon and leave to cool completely, then put in a freezerproof container in the freezer for up to three months. When you're ready to serve, heat the oven to 200°C/180°C fan/400°F/ Gas Mark 6, arrange the frozen potatoes in a single layer in a roasting tin and cook for 35–40 mins until piping hot.

NUTRITIONAL INFO

PER SERVING KCAL **402** | FAT **13G** | SATURATES **5G** | CARBS **62G** | SUGARS **3G** | FIBRE **6G** | PROTEIN **7G** | SALT **0.02G**

✱ V Ve

Ultimate Oven Chips

Prep: 10 mins
Cook: 50 mins

Serves 4

1kg (2lb 4oz) Maris Piper potatoes
1 tsp white wine vinegar or cider vinegar
4 tbsp sunflower oil, plus extra for drizzling
1 tbsp cornflour

1 Heat the oven to 220°C/200°C fan/425°F/Gas Mark 7. Peel the potatoes and chop into medium-sized chips. Rinse under cold running water, then tip into a large pan, cover with cold salted water, add the vinegar and bring to a simmer over a medium heat. Stir once, then continue to simmer for 6–8 mins until the chips are just cooked through but not breaking apart. Drain well. You can now freeze the chips, if you like. Leave them to cool, spread out on a baking tray lined with baking parchment and open-freeze until solid. Transfer to a freezerproof container and freeze for up to three months.

2 Add the oil to a shallow roasting tin and put in the oven to heat for 5 mins. Toss the chips in the cornflour, then carefully tip into the hot oil and arrange in a single layer using tongs. Drizzle with a little more oil to coat, then roast for 20 mins.

3 Carefully turn the chips over in the oil using a spatula, then return to the oven for another 20 mins until golden brown (they might take up to 30 mins if cooking from frozen).

NUTRITIONAL INFO

PER SERVING KCAL **287** | FAT **11G** | SATURATES **1G** | CARBS **41G** | SUGARS **2G** | FIBRE **4G** | PROTEIN **4G** | SALT **0.01G**

✱ V

Prep: 5 mins
Cook: 20 mins

Best Yorkshire Puddings

Makes 8 large puds or 24 small puds

neutral oil (such as vegetable or sunflower), for cooking
140g (5oz) plain flour
4 eggs
200ml (7fl oz) milk

1 Heat the oven to 230°C/210°C fan/450°F/Gas Mark 8. Drizzle a little oil evenly into two four-hole Yorkshire pudding tins or two twelve-hole nonstick muffin tins. Place in the oven to heat through.

2 To make the batter, tip the flour into a bowl and beat in the eggs until smooth. Gradually add the milk and carry on beating until the mix is completely lump free. Season.

3 Pour the batter into a jug. Remove the hot tins from the oven. Carefully and evenly pour the batter into the holes. Take care doing this, as the fat will be sizzling hot. Place the tins back in the oven and leave undisturbed (do not open the oven door!) for 20–25 mins (15–20 mins for smaller puds) until the puddings have puffed up and browned. Serve the Yorkshire puddings immediately.

4 If you're making them in advance, allow them to cool, then transfer to a freezerproof container and pop them in the freezer for up to one month. Reheat from frozen in the oven with your roast, adding them for about 4 mins at the end of the cooking time until hot.

NUTRITIONAL INFO

PER PUDDING (IF MAKING 8 LARGE) KCAL **176** | FAT **10.09G** | SATURATES **2G** | CARBS **15G** | SUGARS **1G** | FIBRE **0.7G** | PROTEIN **6G** | SALT **0.15G**

V

Cauliflower Cheese

Prep: 15 mins
Cook: 1 hr

Serves 4 as a main, 6 as a side

1 large cauliflower, cut into large florets
2 tbsp olive oil
pinch of cayenne pepper
40g (1½oz) parmesan (or vegetarian alternative), finely grated

For the sauce

50g (1¾oz) butter
40g (1½oz) plain flour
600ml (20fl oz) whole milk
1 tsp mustard powder or English mustard
1 tsp yeast extract, such as Marmite (optional)
150g (5½oz) extra-mature cheddar, most grated, the rest cut into small cubes
freshly grated nutmeg

For the topping

3 tbsp dried breadcrumbs (panko work well)
2 tbsp shop-bought crispy onions

1 Heat the oven to 220°C/200°C fan/425°F/Gas Mark 7. Tip the cauliflower into a shallow baking dish and toss with the oil, cayenne pepper and a pinch of salt. Scatter with half the parmesan and roast for 20 mins until crisp and golden. Toss the florets, then sprinkle with more (but not all) of the parmesan and roast for 10 mins more until starting to char a little. Set aside.

2 While the cauliflower is roasting, make the sauce. Heat the butter in a saucepan over a medium heat until frothy. Scatter over and stir in the flour, cooking for 3 mins until you have a sandy paste, then add the milk, a splash at a time, keeping it at a simmer and whisking between each addition until smooth. Once all the milk has been added, continue to cook the sauce gently, stirring occasionally, for 15 mins until thickened and silky. Stir through the mustard and yeast extract, if using. Remove from the heat and add the grated cheddar, a handful at a time, until you have a thick, cheesy sauce. At this point, stir in the cheddar cubes and season with nutmeg, and salt if needed.

3 Pour the sauce over the cauliflower in the baking dish to fully coat it. Mix the breadcrumbs with the remaining parmesan, then scatter this over the cauliflower cheese. You can now keep the dish, once cooled, in the fridge for up to four days.

4 Make sure your oven is still at 220°C/200°C fan/425°F/Gas Mark 7. Bake your cauliflower cheese for 20 mins. Sprinkle with the crispy onions and bake for a further 10 mins until bubbling and deep golden. Serve in warm and melting scoops from the baking dish.

NUTRITIONAL INFO

PER SERVING (IF SERVING 6) KCAL **407** | FAT **27G** | SATURATES **15G** | CARBS **22G** | SUGARS **9G** | FIBRE **3G** | PROTEIN **17G** | SALT **1G**

Green Bean Casserole

✱ V

Prep: 10 mins
Cook: 1 hr

Serves 6 as a side

- 50g (1¾oz) butter
- 2 tbsp olive oil
- 250g (9oz) chestnut or button mushrooms, sliced
- 500g (1lb 2 oz) green beans, trimmed
- 50g (1¾oz) plain flour
- 500ml (18fl oz) milk
- 100g (3½oz) shop-bought crispy onions

1 Heat 1 tbsp of the butter and the oil in a large pan and fry the mushrooms for 10–15 mins until golden. Stir in the green beans and cook for another 3–4 mins until they turn bright green. Scoop out the veg onto a plate.

2 Melt the remaining butter in the pan until foaming. Remove from the heat briefly and sprinkle over the flour, stirring into the butter to make a golden-brown paste. Return to the heat and add the milk, a splash at a time, stirring constantly until all the milk has been added and you have a smooth, thick white sauce. Season well. Stir the beans and mushrooms into the white sauce. Spoon into a medium ovenproof dish. You can now keep the casserole, once cooled, in the fridge for up to two days or in the freezer for up to three months. Defrost in the fridge overnight before continuing.

3 Heat the oven to 200°C/180°C fan/400°F/Gas Mark 6. Scatter over the crispy onions, then bake for 20–30 mins (35 mins if it's been in the fridge) until bubbling and golden, covering with foil if the onions brown too quickly.

NUTRITIONAL INFO

PER SERVING KCAL **311** | FAT **21G** | SATURATES **7G** | CARBS **19G** | SUGARS **6G** | FIBRE **3G** | PROTEIN **9G** | SALT **0.4G**

V

Prep: 15 mins
Cook: 25 mins

Herby Orzo & Lemon Salad

Serves 4–6

- 1 tbsp olive oil
- 1 tbsp butter
- 1 red onion, finely chopped
- 1 garlic clove, finely grated
- ½ tbsp light brown soft sugar
- 350g (12oz) dried orzo
- 50ml (2fl oz) extra virgin olive oil
- juice of 1 large lemon
- small bunch of basil, finely chopped
- small bunch of flat-leaf parsley, finely chopped
- 2 tbsp capers, drained and rinsed
- 50g (1¾oz) flaked almonds, lightly toasted

1 Heat the olive oil and butter in a nonstick frying pan over a medium heat. Fry the onion for 10–15 mins or until golden and caramelized. Add the garlic and sugar and cook for a further 3 mins. Season to taste.

2 Cook the orzo following pack instructions. Drain, then toss with a little of the extra virgin olive oil and leave to cool completely. Whisk the remaining oil with the lemon juice and set aside.

3 Toss the orzo with the caramelized onion and garlic, the lemony dressing, the herbs and capers and half the toasted almonds. Season to taste. Spoon onto a sharing plate and top with the rest of the almonds. Any leftovers can be kept in the fridge for up to three days.

NUTRITIONAL INFO

PER SERVING (IF SERVING 6) KCAL **410** | FAT **18G** | SATURATES **3G** | CARBS **50G** | SUGARS **5G** | FIBRE **3G** | PROTEIN **12G** | SALT **0.4G**

V

Prep: 15 mins
Cook: 6 mins

Crunchy Broccoli, Cranberry & Halloumi Salad

Serves 4

2 tbsp Dijon mustard
juice of 1 lemon
1 tbsp apple cider vinegar
1 tbsp honey
1 tsp garlic granules
4 tbsp cold-pressed rapeseed oil or mild olive oil
1 head of broccoli (about 350g/12oz), cut into florets
150g (5½oz) kale
200g (7oz) halloumi, cut into 1cm (½ inch) thick slices
50g (1¾oz) dried cranberries
40g (1½oz) mixed seeds
50g (1¾oz) roasted, salted pecans, roughly chopped

1 First, make the dressing. Spoon the mustard, lemon juice, vinegar, honey, garlic granules and oil into a screw-top jar. Seal and shake well until emulsified, then season to taste.

2 Chop the broccoli florets into bite-size pieces. Finely chop the stalk. Add both to a large bowl. Strip the kale leaves from the stalks and roughly chop. Finely chop the kale stalks. Add both to the bowl with the broccoli.

3 Heat a nonstick pan over a medium–high heat. Add the halloumi and fry on both sides for 2–3 mins until golden brown, then transfer to a chopping board and roughly chop. Mix with the kale and broccoli. Add most of the cranberries, seeds and pecans and mix again. Transfer to an airtight container, with a layer of kitchen paper on top, and set aside until you're ready to serve.

4 To serve, transfer the salad to a serving bowl and drizzle over the dressing. Toss together well, then scatter over the remaining cranberries, seeds and pecans. Keep any leftovers in the fridge for a delicious lunch the next day.

NUTRITIONAL INFO

PER SERVING KCAL **577** | FAT **43G** | SATURATES **11G** | CARBS **23G** | SUGARS **17G** | FIBRE **8G** | PROTEIN **22G** | SALT **2.57G**

V

Easy Quinoa Salad

Prep: 30 mins
Cook: 30 mins

Serves 4

200g (7oz) quinoa

1 red onion, peeled but left whole, then cut into 1cm(½ inch) thick round slices

2 peppers, red, yellow or a mixture, cut into chunky long wedges

3 tbsp olive oil

200g (7oz) baby courgettes, halved lengthways

3 garlic cloves, unpeeled

zest and juice of 1 lemon

pinch of golden caster sugar

small pack of flat-leaf parsley, roughly chopped

200g (7oz) feta

1 Cook the quinoa following pack instructions, then drain really well and set aside.

2 Meanwhile, heat the oven to 200°C/180°C fan/400°F/Gas Mark 6. Toss the onion and peppers with 1 tbsp of the oil and some seasoning on a roasting tray, then roast for 15 mins.

3 Add the courgettes and garlic cloves, toss with the rest of the veg and roast for another 15 mins.

4 Squeeze the roasted garlic cloves out of their skins and mash with some seasoning. Stir in the remaining oil and the lemon zest and juice and season with sugar to taste. Drizzle the dressing over the quinoa, then toss together with the roasted vegetables. Add the parsley, crumble over the feta, toss gently again and serve.

5 This salad keeps well in the fridge, so you can make it ahead of time and keep any leftovers chilled for lunch the next day.

NUTRITIONAL INFO

PER SERVING KCAL **404** | FAT **21.4G** | SATURATES **8.4G** | CARBS **35.3G** | SUGARS **11.2G** | FIBRE **2.6G** | PROTEIN **17.3G** | SALT **1.9G**

V

Tangy Cabbage Slaw

Prep: 15 mins

Makes enough for 12–16 pulled pork buns

250ml (9fl oz) mayonnaise
zest and juice of 1 lemon
2 tbsp cider vinegar
2 tbsp wholegrain mustard
1 tsp celery salt
¼ head of white cabbage, very thinly sliced
¼ head of red cabbage, very thinly sliced
2 carrots, julienned
1 large red onion, finely chopped
2 celery sticks, thinly sliced

TIP

This coleslaw is delicious with the Pulled Pork on page 95.

1 Whisk together the mayonnaise, lemon zest and juice, the vinegar, mustard and celery salt in a small bowl. Season generously.

2 Put the cabbage, carrots, onion and celery in a large bowl. Pour the dressing over and mix well. Cover and put in the fridge until needed. The slaw can be made up to 24 hrs in advance and any leftovers keep well in the fridge for finishing up the next day.

NUTRITIONAL INFO

PER SERVING (IF SERVING 16) KCAL **262** | FAT **24G** | SATURATES **4G** | CARBS **8G** | SUGARS **7G** | FIBRE **3G** | PROTEIN **2G** | SALT **1.3G**

✱ V Ve

Prep: 10 mins

No-Cook Chickpea Salad

Serves 6

400g (14oz) can chickpeas, drained and rinsed
small pack of coriander, roughly chopped
small pack of flat-leaf parsley, roughly chopped
1 red onion, thinly sliced
2 large tomatoes, chopped
2 tbsp olive oil
2 tbsp harissa
juice of 1 lemon

1. Mix all the ingredients together in a bowl, mashing everything a little so that the chickpeas are a bit rough round the edges – this helps absorb the dressing.
2. This salad keeps well in the fridge, so you can make it ahead of time and keep any leftovers chilled for lunch the next day.

NUTRITIONAL INFO

PER SERVING KCAL **111** | FAT **5G** | SATURATES **1G** | CARBS **10G** | SUGARS **3G** | FIBRE **4G** | PROTEIN **4G** | SALT **0.09G**

Desserts

✱ V

Prep: 20 mins
Cook: 1 hr and 10 mins

Sunken Chocolate, Olive Oil & Hazelnut Cake

Serves 8–10

- 100g (3½oz) blanched hazelnuts, roughly chopped
- 175ml (6fl oz) extra virgin olive oil, plus extra for oiling
- 200g (7oz) dark chocolate (70% cocoa solids), roughly chopped
- 5 eggs, separated
- 175g (6oz) golden caster sugar

To serve

- 1 tbsp icing sugar
- scoops of vanilla ice cream (optional)

1. Heat a dry frying pan over a medium heat and tip in the hazelnuts. Toast, shaking the pan from time to time, until golden and fragrant. Transfer to a plate to cool completely, then tip into a food processor and blitz until finely chopped, like breadcrumbs. Alternatively, you can use a mini chopper or the chopper attachment on a hand blender.
2. Oil and line the base and sides of a 23cm (9 inch) springform cake tin. Tip the chocolate into a heatproof bowl and set over a pan of just-simmering water, making sure the base of the bowl doesn't touch the water, until melted, giving it a stir every now and then. Alternatively, melt in 20-second blasts in the microwave. Once fully melted, remove from the heat and slowly pour in the olive oil, whisking constantly until the mixture is smooth and glossy.
3. Beat the egg yolks and 50g (1¾oz) of the caster sugar in another bowl for about 5 mins until pale and thickened. Gently fold the whisked yolk mixture into the chocolate mixture along with the chopped hazelnuts and a pinch of sea salt. (The ingredients don't need to be fully combined yet.) Set aside.
4. Whisk the egg whites and remaining sugar together in a separate bowl, using a stand mixer or an electric whisk until medium-soft peaks form. Use a large metal spoon to stir a little of the whisked egg whites into the chocolate mixture to loosen, then gently fold in the remainder. Carefully pour the batter into the prepared tin. The cake mix will now keep, wrapped, in the freezer for up to two months.
5. If you're cooking immediately, heat the oven to 180°C/160°C fan/350°F/Gas Mark 4 and bake for 35–45 mins. To cook from frozen, heat the oven as above, but bake for 55 mins–1 hr until a skewer inserted into the middle comes out almost clean, with just a few crumbs clinging to it. Leave to cool in the tin until just warm, then carefully remove the base and sides of the tin. Dust with the icing sugar and serve with scoops of vanilla ice cream, if you like.

NUTRITIONAL INFO

PER SERVING (IF SERVING 10) KCAL **448** | FAT **35G** | SATURATES **9G** | CARBS **25G** | SUGARS **23G** | FIBRE **3G** | PROTEIN **7G** | SALT **0.1G**

Rhubarb Crumble

✻ V

Prep: 20 mins
Cook: 45 mins

Serves 6

800g (1lb 12oz) rhubarb, chopped into roughly 5cm (2 inch) pieces

50g (1¾oz) golden caster sugar

1 tsp vanilla extract

1 tsp cornflour

custard, cream or ice cream, to serve

For the topping

200g (7oz) self-raising flour

50g (1¾oz) custard powder

150g (5½oz) salted butter, cut into small pieces

125g (4½oz) golden caster sugar

25g (1oz) demerara sugar

1 To make the crumble topping, tip the flour, custard powder and butter into a large bowl, then rub together using your fingertips until the mixture resembles coarse breadcrumbs. Stir in both the sugars. You can now keep the crumble topping in the fridge for up to three days or in the freezer for up to three months. When you're ready to use the topping, break it up with your hands before using. If using straight from the fridge, the topping will be a bit chunkier. If you prefer it to be looser, leave it to come back to room temperature before using.

2 Toss the rhubarb, sugar, vanilla extract and cornflour together in a large bowl, ensuring the rhubarb pieces are evenly coated. Set aside to macerate for 30 mins. Tip the rhubarb into a large ovenproof baking dish and spread into an even layer. Sprinkle over the crumble topping, making sure it covers the rhubarb completely. You can now put the crumble in the fridge for up to 24 hours until you're ready to bake or in the freezer for up to three months. Defrost completely in the fridge overnight before continuing.

3 Heat the oven to 200°C/180°C fan/400°F/Gas Mark 6. Bake the crumble for 40–45 mins until the topping is golden and crisp and the rhubarb filling is bubbling at the edges. Leave to cool for 10 mins before serving with your choice of custard, cream or ice cream.

NUTRITIONAL INFO

PER SERVING KCAL **490** | FAT **21G** | SATURATES **13G** | CARBS **68G** | SUGARS **35G** | FIBRE **4G** | PROTEIN **5G** | SALT **0.83G**

✱ V

Prep: 1 hr
Cook: 25 mins

Ultimate Sticky Toffee Pudding

Makes 7 little puddings

85g (3oz) butter, softened, plus extra for the tins
175g (6oz) self-raising flour, plus extra for the tins
225g (8oz) whole medjool dates, stoned and chopped into small pieces
1 tsp vanilla extract
1 tsp bicarbonate of soda
2 eggs
140g (5oz) demerara sugar
2 tbsp black treacle
100ml (3½fl oz) milk
cream or custard, to serve (optional)

For the toffee sauce

175g (6oz) light muscovado sugar
50g (1¾oz) butter, cut into pieces
225ml (8fl oz) double cream
1 tbsp black treacle

NUTRITIONAL INFO

PER SERVING KCAL **697** | FAT **36G** | SATURATES **21G** | CARBS **92G** | SUGARS **71G** | FIBRE **2G** | PROTEIN **6G** | SALT **1.1G**

1. Butter and flour seven mini pudding tins (each about 200ml/7fl oz) and sit them on a baking sheet. Heat the oven to 180°C/160°C fan/350°F/Gas Mark 4. Put the dates in a heatproof bowl and pour over 175ml (6fl oz) boiling water. Leave for about 30 mins until cool and well soaked, then mash a bit with a fork. Stir in the vanilla extract.
2. Meanwhile, make the puddings. Mix the flour and bicarbonate of soda together in a bowl. Beat the eggs in a separate bowl.
3. Beat the softened butter and demerara sugar together in a large bowl for a few minutes until slightly creamy (the mixture will be grainy). Add the eggs one at a time, beating well between each addition. Beat in the black treacle. Using a large metal spoon, gently fold in one-third of the flour and bicarbonate of soda mixture, then half the milk, being careful not to overbeat. Repeat until all the flour mixture and all the milk has been added. Stir in the soaked dates. The mixture may look a little curdled at this point and will be like a soft, thick batter. Spoon it evenly between the prepared tins and bake for 20–25 mins until risen and firm.
4. Meanwhile, make the toffee sauce. Put the sugar and butter in a medium saucepan with half the double cream. Bring to the boil over a medium heat, stirring constantly, until the sugar has completely dissolved. Stir in the black treacle, then turn up the heat slightly and let the mixture bubble away for 2–3 mins until it is a rich toffee colour. Stir occasionally to make sure it doesn't burn. Take the pan off the heat and beat in the rest of the cream.
5. Remove the puddings from the oven. Leave in the tins for a few minutes, then loosen them from the sides of the tins with a small palette knife before turning them out.
6. You can serve them now with the sauce drizzled over, but they'll be even stickier if left for a day or two coated in the sauce. Pour half the sauce into one or two ovenproof dishes. Sit the upturned puddings on the sauce, then pour over the rest of the sauce. Cover with a loose tent of foil (there's no need to keep them in the fridge). Or you can freeze them for up to three months – defrost before continuing.
7. When you're ready to serve, heat the oven to 180°C/160°C fan/350°F/Gas Mark 4. Warm the puddings through, still covered, for 15–20 mins or until the sauce is bubbling. Serve them on their own, or with a drizzle of cream or custard.

✻ V

Prep: 20 mins
Cook: 35 mins

Squidgy Chocolate Pear Pudding

Serves 8

200g (7oz) butter, plus extra for the dish
300g (10½oz) golden caster sugar
4 large eggs
75g (2¾oz) plain flour
50g (1¾oz) cocoa powder
410g (14½oz) pears, peeled, halved and cored
100g (3½oz) dark chocolate (70% cocoa solids)
25g (1oz) flaked almonds (optional)
cream or ice cream, to serve

1. Lightly butter a shallow ovenproof dish, about 20 x 30cm (8 x 12 inches). Put the butter in a large saucepan and place over a low heat until just melted. Remove from the heat and stir in the sugar until well combined.
2. Whisk the eggs together in a large bowl. Gradually add the eggs to the butter and sugar, beating well with a wooden spoon in between each addition. Sift the flour and cocoa powder on top of the egg mixture, then beat hard with a wooden spoon until thoroughly combined.
3. Pour into the prepared dish and nestle the pears into the chocolate batter. Put the dark chocolate on a chopping board and, using a large knife, cut it into chunky pieces, each roughly 1.5cm (⅝ inch). Scatter the chocolate pieces over the batter and sprinkle with the flaked almonds too, if you like. If not eating immediately, you can now freeze the unbaked pudding for up to one month, wrapped tightly in foil. When you're ready to serve, unwrap the pudding and bake from frozen.
4. Heat the oven to 190°C/170°C fan/375°F/Gas Mark 5. Bake in the centre of the oven for 30 mins (50 mins from frozen) or until the mixture is crusty on the surface and lightly cooked inside. Do not allow to overcook, as the cake will become spongy rather than gooey in the centre. Serve warm with cream or ice cream.

NUTRITIONAL INFO

PER SERVING KCAL **513** | FAT **30G** | SATURATES **17G** | CARBS **53G** | SUGARS **43G** | FIBRE **4G** | PROTEIN **6G** | SALT **1G**

✱ V

Prep: 20 mins, plus freezing

Chocolate Ice Cream

Serves 6–8

200g (7oz) dark chocolate (at least 70% cocoa solids), chopped into small pieces
500ml (18fl oz) double cream
340g (11¾oz) can sweetened condensed milk
1 tsp vanilla extract
3 tbsp organic cocoa powder, sifted
50g (1¾oz) milk chocolate chips
flaky sea salt, to serve (optional)

1 Melt the chocolate in a heatproof bowl set over a pan of just-simmering water, ensuring the base of the bowl doesn't touch the water. Alternatively, melt the chocolate in the microwave in 20-second blasts until smooth and glossy. Leave to cool slightly.

2 Pour the cream, condensed milk and vanilla extract into a separate bowl and beat for 3 mins using an electric whisk until slightly thickened and the beaters leave a trail in the mixture when lifted across the bowl. Be careful not to overwhip, as you don't want the mixture to be too stiff – as soon as the beaters leave a trail, it's ready.

3 Gently fold the melted chocolate and cocoa powder into the cream mixture until thoroughly combined, ensuring the spatula is reaching the bottom of the bowl so that all the chocolate gets mixed in. Fold in most of the chocolate chips, reserving a small handful. Scrape the mixture into a 1 litre (1¾ pint) freezerproof container, then scatter over the reserved chocolate chips. Cover and freeze for at least 6 hrs until firm but scoopable. The ice cream will keep in the freezer for up to one month.

4 To serve, scoop the ice cream into chilled bowls or ice cream cones and sprinkle with a pinch of flaky sea salt, if you like.

NUTRITIONAL INFO

PER SERVING (IF SERVING 8) KCAL **642** | FAT **51G** | SATURATES **31G** | CARBS **36G** | SUGARS **33G** | FIBRE **4G** | PROTEIN **8G** | SALT **0.2G**

V

Prep: 20 mins
Cook: 1 hr

Chocolate Orange Brownie Tart

Serves 6–8

320g (11¼oz) pack of ready-rolled shortcrust pastry

120g (4¼oz) butter, cut into cubes

120g (4¼oz) dark chocolate (at least 70% cocoa solids), chopped

2 eggs

80g (2¾oz) golden caster sugar

80g (2¾oz) light brown soft sugar

80g (2¾oz) plain flour

zest and juice of 1 orange, plus a little more zest to serve

crème fraîche, to serve

1. Heat the oven to 180°C/160°C fan/350°F/Gas Mark 4. Use the shortcrust pastry sheet to line a 20cm (8 inch) tart tin. Press into the sides of the tin and loosely cut around the edges, leaving a little overhanging. Line the pastry with a scrunched-up piece of baking parchment and fill with raw rice or baking beans. Bake for 15 mins, then remove the parchment and rice or baking beans and bake for another 5–10 mins until dry.
2. While the pastry is cooking, put the butter and chocolate into a heatproof bowl set over a pan of just-simmering water and melt together, stirring often. Once fully melted, remove from the heat and leave to cool slightly. Add a pinch of salt if your butter is unsalted.
3. Whisk together the eggs and both sugars briefly in a bowl until combined, then stir in the melted chocolate and butter. Sift the flour over and fold in until just combined. Stir in the orange zest and juice.
4. Trim the edges of the pastry tart with a serrated knife to neaten, then spoon the brownie mixture into the middle. Smooth over with the back of a spoon or spatula and bake for 30–35 mins until the top forms a crust and the filling is no longer wet but slightly wobbly.
5. Leave to cool for 15 mins before removing from the tin if serving warm. Or leave it to cool completely and serve at room temperature. Serve with a dollop of crème fraîche and some more orange zest grated over. Any leftovers will keep for three days in an airtight container.

NUTRITIONAL INFO

PER SERVING (IF SERVING 8) KCAL **512** | FAT **31G** | SATURATES **18G** | CARBS **49G** | SUGARS **24G** | FIBRE **3G** | PROTEIN **6G** | SALT **0.4G**

✱ V

Prep: 20 mins, plus freezing
Cook: 3 mins

Raspberry & Dark Chocolate Ice Cream Terrine

Serves 8–10

225g (8oz) raspberries
1 tbsp golden caster sugar
juice of ½ a lemon
400ml (14fl oz) double cream
1 tbsp vanilla paste
275g (9¾oz) condensed milk
200g (7oz) dark chocolate (at least 70% cocoa solids), melted and cooled slightly, plus extra for the topping

1 Line a 900g (2lb) loaf tin (ours was 9 x 20 x 7cm/3½ x 8 x 2¾ inches) with two sheets of overlapping baking parchment, leaving quite a bit overhanging on all sides of the tin – preferably enough to pull up to cover the top of the tin. Put 175g (6oz) of the raspberries, the caster sugar and the lemon juice in a pan over a medium heat and simmer for 3 mins until softened slightly. Tip into a food processor or use a hand blender to blitz until smooth.

2 Whisk the cream, vanilla paste and condensed milk together in a bowl using an electric whisk until soft peaks form. Pour in the raspberry purée, then stir carefully a few times to marble the raspberry through the cream mixture.

3 Tip the remaining raspberries into the base of the lined tin. Cover with a third of the cream mixture, spreading it out evenly. Tap the tin down on a surface so that the mixture covers the raspberries. Using a spoon, drizzle over half the melted chocolate to cover the cream. Top with another third of the cream mixture and spread it out. Drizzle over the remaining chocolate and top with the remaining cream mixture.

4 Use the overhanging parchment to cover the top of the tin, using more parchment if it doesn't cover the terrine completely, and freeze for at least 8 hrs or overnight. Before serving, let the ice cream sit at room temperature for 10 mins. Tip upside down and remove from the tin. Drizzle with a little more melted chocolate to decorate. Run boiling water over your knife, wipe dry and slice the terrine to serve. Any leftovers can be returned to the freezer for another day.

NUTRITIONAL INFO

PER SERVING (IF SERVING 10) KCAL **416** | FAT **31G** | SATURATES **19G** | CARBS **28G** | SUGARS **26G** | FIBRE **2G** | PROTEIN **4G** | SALT **0.1G**

✱ V

Prep: 20 mins
Cook: 25 mins

Classic Bread & Butter Pudding

Serves 6–8

600ml (20fl oz) double cream
8 large egg yolks
175g (6oz) golden caster sugar, plus extra for the topping
16 slices of white bread, crusts removed
75g (2¾oz) unsalted butter, softened
100g (3½oz) raisins
¼–½ whole nutmeg
ice cream, to serve (optional)

1 Heat the cream gently in a pan until boiling. Meanwhile, whisk the egg yolks and sugar together in a large bowl using an electric whisk for 3–5 mins until light and fluffy. Pour the hot cream over the eggs, whisking constantly. When the custard is mixed, set it aside.

2 Spread the bread with the butter and cut into triangles. Arrange in a shallow baking dish, measuring about 20 x 26 x 5cm (8 x 10½ x 2 inches), buttered-side up, in three layers. Sprinkle the raisins and a fine grating of nutmeg over the bottom two layers, leaving the top layer clear. Pour over the warm custard, lightly pressing the bread down with your fingers to help it soak in. Leave to stand for at least 20 mins before cooking. You can now chill your pudding for a few hours until you're ready to cook.

3 Heat the oven to 180°C/160°C fan/350°F/Gas Mark 4. Sit the dish in a large roasting tin and pour a kettleful of hot water into the tin so that it comes three-quarters of the way up the outside of the dish. Bake in the oven for 20–25 mins until the custard is just set.

4 Remove the pudding dish from its water bath and scatter the top liberally with more sugar. Caramelize the top under a hot grill or with a blowtorch – take it really far (a few burnt edges add to the flavour) but be careful it doesn't catch. You can now freeze the pudding if you like. Leave to cool completely, then cover and freeze for up to three months. Defrost in the fridge overnight, then reheat in the oven at 180°C/160°C fan/350°F/ Gas Mark 4 for 10–15 mins until hot.

5 If serving immediately, leave the pudding to rest for 5 mins, then serve with your favourite ice cream, if you like.

NUTRITIONAL INFO

PER SERVING (IF SERVING 8) KCAL **743** | FAT **54G** | SATURATES **32G** | CARBS **53G** | SUGARS **33G** | FIBRE **2G** | PROTEIN **9G** | SALT **0.5G**

Bakes

✳ V

Prep: 5 mins
Cook: 50 mins–1 hr

Chocolate Chip Banana Bread

Serves 8–10

140g (5oz) unsalted butter, softened, plus extra for the tin
140g (5oz) golden caster sugar
2 eggs, beaten
1 tsp vanilla extract
140g (5oz) self-raising flour
1 tsp baking powder
3 ripe bananas, peeled and mashed
100g (3½oz) chocolate chips

1 Heat the oven to 180°C/160°C fan/350°F/Gas Mark 4. Butter a 900g (2lb) loaf tin and line the base and sides with baking parchment.

2 Beat the softened butter and sugar together in a bowl using an electric whisk until light and fluffy. Combine the eggs and vanilla extract and pour this in, a little at a time, mixing between each addition. Fold in the flour, a pinch of salt, the baking powder, mashed bananas and most of the chocolate chips. Scrape the mixture into the prepared tin and scatter over the rest of the chocolate chips.

3 Bake for about 50 mins or until puffed up and cooked through – a skewer inserted into the middle of the loaf should come out clean. Leave to cool in the tin for 10 mins, then remove to a wire rack and leave to cool completely. Slice before serving. The banana bread will keep in an airtight container for up to five days. It can also be frozen, with individual slices wrapped in baking parchment, for up to three months. Defrost thoroughly at room temperature before serving.

NUTRITIONAL INFO

PER SERVING (IF SERVING 10) KCAL **306** | FAT **17G** | SATURATES **10G** | CARBS **34G** | SUGARS **22G** | FIBRE **2G** | PROTEIN **4G** | SALT **0.29G**

✱ V

Vanilla Cupcakes

Prep: 20 mins
Cook: 15 mins

Makes 12

110g (3¾oz) butter, softened
110g (3¾oz) golden caster sugar
2 large eggs
½ tsp vanilla extract
110g (3¾oz) self-raising flour

For the buttercream

150g (5½oz) butter, softened
300g (10½oz) icing sugar
1 tsp vanilla extract
3 tbsp milk
food colouring paste of your choice (optional)

1 Heat the oven to 180°C/160°C fan/350°F/Gas Mark 4. Fill a 12-hole cupcake tin with paper cupcake cases.

2 To make the sponge, beat the softened butter and golden caster sugar together in a bowl using an electric whisk until pale and fluffy. Whisk in the eggs, one at a time, scraping down the sides of the bowl after each addition. Add the vanilla extract, flour and a pinch of salt. Whisk until just combined, then spoon the mixture into the cupcake cases.

3 Bake for 15 mins until golden brown and a skewer inserted into the middle of each cake comes out clean. Leave to cool completely on a wire rack.

4 To make the buttercream, whisk the softened butter until in a bowl super soft, then add the icing sugar, vanilla extract and a pinch of salt. Whisk together until smooth (start off slowly to avoid an icing sugar cloud), then beat in the milk.

5 If you want to colour your buttercream, stir in the food colouring now. Then spoon or pipe onto the cooled cupcakes. The cupcakes can be eaten straight away or frozen (without the buttercream icing) in a freezerproof container for up to three months. Defrost thoroughly at room temperature before eating.

NUTRITIONAL INFO

PER CUPCAKE KCAL **350** | FAT **19G** | SATURATES **12G** | CARBS **41G** | SUGARS **34G** | FIBRE **0.4G** | PROTEIN **3G** | SALT **0.6G**

✱ V

Carrot Cake

Prep: 30 mins
Cook: 45 mins

Makes 15 slices

175ml (6fl oz) sunflower oil, plus extra for the tin

175g (6oz) light muscovado sugar

3 large eggs, lightly beaten

140g (5oz) carrots (about 3 medium), grated

100g (3½oz) raisins

zest of 1 large orange

175g (6oz) self-raising flour

1 tsp bicarbonate of soda

1 tsp ground cinnamon

½ tsp grated nutmeg (freshly grated will give you the best flavour)

For the frosting

175g (6oz) icing sugar

1½–2 tbsp orange juice

1 Heat the oven to 180°C/160°C fan/350°F/Gas Mark 4. Oil and line the base and sides of an 18cm (7 inch) square cake tin with baking parchment.

2 Tip the oil, muscovado sugar and eggs into a large mixing bowl. Lightly mix with a wooden spoon. Stir in the grated carrots, raisins and orange zest. Sift the flour, bicarbonate of soda, cinnamon and nutmeg into the bowl. Mix everything together – the mixture will be soft and almost runny.

3 Pour the mixture into the prepared tin and bake for 40–45 mins or until it feels firm and springy when you press it in the centre. Cool in the tin for 5 mins, then turn out the cake, peel off the paper and cool on a wire rack. You can freeze the cake in a freezerproof container for up to three months at this point. Defrost thoroughly at room temperature before continuing.

4 To make the frosting, beat the icing sugar and orange juice together in a bowl until smooth – you want the icing about as runny as single cream. Boldly drizzle the icing back and forth in diagonal lines over the top, letting it drip down the sides.

NUTRITIONAL INFO

PER SERVING KCAL **279** | FAT **13G** | SATURATES **2G** | CARBS **37G** | SUGARS **28G** | FIBRE **1G** | PROTEIN **3G** | SALT **0.4G**

✻ V

Prep: 20 mins
Cook: 12–15 mins

Chocolate Drop Cookies

Makes 14–16

75g (2¾oz) dark brown soft sugar
75g (2¾oz) light brown soft sugar
100g (3½oz) golden caster sugar
150g (5½oz) unsalted butter, softened
1 egg
1 tsp vanilla extract
260g (9¼oz) plain flour
1 tsp bicarbonate of soda
190g (6¾oz) sugar-coated chocolate drops, such as Smarties, half lightly crushed, half left whole
10g (¼oz) freeze-dried raspberry pieces (optional)
multi-coloured sprinkles, to decorate (optional)

1 Beat the sugars and butter together either in a bowl using an electric whisk or in a stand mixer fitted with the paddle attachment for 3–4 mins until lighter in colour. Add the egg and vanilla extract, then mix again until fully combined.

2 Scrape down the sides of the bowl and stir in the flour, bicarbonate of soda and ¾ tsp salt. Fold everything together until mostly combined, then add the lightly crushed chocolate drops and the freeze-dried raspberry pieces, if using. Mix until these are evenly dispersed throughout the dough.

3 Shape the dough into 14–16 equal balls (about 60g/2¼oz each), then gently press 3–4 whole sugar-coated chocolate drops and some sprinkles, if using, into each one. Transfer to a baking sheet lined with baking parchment and chill for at least 1 hr, or overnight for best results. The cookies can be baked straight away, but they will spread more if they haven't been chilled. You can also freeze some or all of the cookies at this stage – simply transfer to a freezerproof container and freeze for up to three months.

4 Heat the oven to 180° C/160° C fan/350° F/Gas Mark 4 and bake the cookies for 12–15 mins (15–17 mins from frozen) until golden and still slightly soft in the middle. Cool completely on a wire rack before serving. The cookies will keep in an airtight container for up to five days or in the freezer for up to three months. Defrost completely at room temperature before serving.

NUTRITIONAL INFO

PER SERVING (IF MAKING 16) KCAL **252** | FAT **10G** | SATURATES **6G** | CARBS **36G** | SUGARS **23G** | FIBRE **1G** | PROTEIN **3G** | SALT **0.44G**

V

Prep: 20 mins
Cook: 20 mins

Easy Blueberry Muffins

Makes 12

- 100g (3½oz) unsalted butter, softened, plus 1 tbsp, melted, for greasing
- 140g (5oz) golden caster sugar
- 2 large eggs
- 140ml (4½fl oz) natural yogurt
- 1 tsp vanilla extract
- 2 tbsp milk
- 250g (9oz) plain flour
- 2 tsp baking powder
- 1 tsp bicarbonate of soda
- 125g (4½oz) blueberries, fresh or frozen

1 Heat the oven to 200°C/180°C fan/400°F/Gas Mark 6 and line a 12-hole muffin tin with paper cases. Beat the butter and sugar together in a bowl until pale and fluffy. Add the eggs and beat for 1 min, then mix in the yogurt, vanilla extract and milk.

2 Combine the flour, baking powder and bicarbonate of soda in a separate bowl with ¼ tsp fine salt, then tip this into the wet ingredients and stir in. Finally, fold in the blueberries, then divide the mixture between the muffin cases.

3 Bake for 5 mins, then reduce the oven to 180°C/160°C fan/350°F/Gas Mark 4 and bake for 15–18 mins more until risen and golden and a cocktail stick inserted into the middle of each muffin comes out clean.

4 Cool in the tin for 10 mins, then carefully lift out onto a wire rack to finish cooling. The muffins will keep for up to four days in an airtight container – after a day or two, pop them in the microwave for 10–15 seconds on full power to freshen up before eating.

NUTRITIONAL INFO

PER MUFFIN KCAL **226** | FAT **10G** | SATURATES **6G** | CARBS **30G** | SUGARS **14G** | FIBRE **1G** | PROTEIN **4G** | SALT **0.6G**

✳ V

Next-Level Mince Pies

Prep: 40 mins, plus chilling
Cook: 30 mins

Makes 12

For the mincemeat

100g (3½oz) dark muscovado sugar
50g (1¾oz) unsalted butter
1 cooking apple, peeled, cored and coarsely grated
150g (5½oz) currants
150g (5½oz) sultanas
100g (3½oz) raisins
75g (2¾oz) candied mixed peel, chopped
zest and juice of 1 lemon
1½ tsp ground mixed spice
1 tsp ground cinnamon
100ml (3½fl oz) Pedro Ximénez sherry, brandy, rum or whisky

For the pastry

300g (10½oz) self-raising flour, plus extra for dusting
1 tbsp cornflour
2 tbsp granulated sugar, plus extra for the tins and topping
zest of 1 orange, tangerine or clementine
175g (6oz) unsalted butter, 150g (5½oz) cold and cut into small pieces, the rest melted for the tin
150g (5½oz) soft cheese
1 egg, beaten, to glaze

To serve (optional)

icing sugar

NUTRITIONAL INFO

PER SERVING KCAL **318** | FAT **17G** | SATURATES **10G** | CARBS **36G** | SUGARS **16G** | FIBRE **2G** | PROTEIN **4G** | SALT **0.71G**

1 To make the mincemeat, tip the sugar and butter into a frying pan or shallow pan and melt over a medium heat until the sugar has dissolved into a bubbling caramel. Stir through the apple to coat. Over a low heat, stir through all the other mincemeat ingredients, except the alcohol, and cook for 7–8 mins or until the dried fruit has plumped up. Remove the pan from the heat and stir through the alcohol. Leave to cool, then give it another good stir.

2 To store the mincemeat, spoon it into sterilized jars while still warm and seal. This will keep in a cool, dry place for up to six months.

3 To make the pastry, tip both flours and the sugar into a bowl with the orange zest and a large pinch of salt. Use your fingers to rub the butter pieces into the flour mixture until it resembles coarse breadcrumbs, then rub in the soft cheese until the pastry comes together. If it's still crumbly, add 1 tbsp iced water and it should come together.

4 Tip the dough onto a work surface and knead for 30 seconds. Wrap and chill for at least 1 hr.

5 Heat the oven to 220°C/200°C fan/425°F/Gas Mark 7. Brush the holes of a 12-hole muffin tin with the melted butter, then lightly sprinkle with extra sugar. Roll out the pastry on a floured work surface until 5mm (¼ inch) thick. Stamp out 12 circles using a 10cm (4 inch) round cutter (a fluted edge looks nice but is not essential), re-rolling offcuts if needed, and use to line the base and sides of each hole of the muffin tin. Scoop some mincemeat into each pastry case until it's a little below the rim.

6 Lightly brush the edges of the pastry cases with some of the beaten egg. Roll out the remaining pastry on a floured work surface and use a 6cm (2½ inch) round cutter to stamp out 12 more circles for the lids (again, a fluted edge looks nice but is not essential) and gently press on the lids to seal. Brush over the rest of the egg and sprinkle over more sugar. Bake for 15–20 mins until deep golden. Remove from the oven and leave to cool for just a few minutes. While still quite hot, twist them out of their holes and put on a wire rack to cool a bit more.

7 The mince pies are best served warm, dusted with icing sugar, if you like. Alternatively, leave them to cool completely, transfer to an airtight container and keep at room temperature for up to three days or in the freezer for up to three months. Defrost thoroughly before eating.

✱ V

Prep: 20 mins
Cook: 1 hr and 10 mins

Spiced Plum & Coconut Cake

Serves 12

200g (7oz) butter, melted
200ml (7fl oz) Greek-style coconut-flavoured yogurt, plus extra to serve (optional)
200g (7oz) light brown soft sugar, plus an extra 1 tbsp for the topping
3 eggs
1 tsp vanilla extract
250g (9oz) self-raising flour
85g (3oz) desiccated coconut
½ tsp baking powder
1 tsp ground mixed spice
1 tsp ground cinnamon
4 plums, halved, stoned and cut into wedges
handful of coconut flakes or extra desiccated coconut (optional)

1 Heat the oven to 180°C/160°C fan/350°F/Gas Mark 4 and line a 20cm (8 inch) springform cake tin with baking parchment. Whisk together the melted butter, yogurt, sugar, eggs and vanilla extract in a jug to combine. Mix together the flour, desiccated coconut, baking powder, spices and ½ tsp salt in a bowl.

2 Pour the wet ingredients into the dry and mix into a smooth batter. Pour into the lined tin, then arrange the plums on top. Scatter over the 1 tbsp sugar and coconut flakes or desiccated coconut, if using. Bake for 1 hr 10 mins or until risen, golden and a skewer inserted into the middle of the cake comes out clean.

3 Leave to cool in the tin for 15 mins, then transfer to a wire rack to cool a little more. Serve warm with a spoonful of coconut yogurt, if you like. Alternatively, leave to cool completely and transfer to an airtight container. The cake will keep at room temperature for up to three days or in the freezer for up to three months, slices wrapped in baking parchment. Defrost thoroughly at room temperature before eating.

NUTRITIONAL INFO

PER SERVING KCAL **356** | FAT **21G** | SATURATES **14G** | CARBS **36G** | SUGARS **20G** | FIBRE **3G** | PROTEIN **5G** | SALT **0.8G**

✱ V

Prep: 10 mins
Cook: 25 mins

Raspberry Honey Flapjacks

Makes 9–12

150g (5½oz) butter
150g (5½oz) light brown soft sugar
4 tbsp honey (we used heather honey)
300g (10½oz) porridge oats
100g (3½oz) frozen raspberries

1 Heat the oven to 200°C/180°C fan/400°F/Gas Mark 6 and line a 20cm (8 inch) square baking tin with baking parchment. Melt the butter, sugar, honey and a pinch of salt in a pan. Once the mixture is bubbling and combined, stir in the oats.

2 Tip the oat mixture into the lined baking tin and press down with the back of a spoon. Scatter over the raspberries, then lightly press them into the oat mixture. Bake for 25–30 mins until golden brown. Remove from the oven and leave to cool, then cut into nine or twelve flapjacks and serve. Any leftovers can be kept in an airtight container for up to three days. Or you can freeze the squares, wrapped individually in baking parchment, for up to three months. Defrost thoroughly at room temperature before eating.

NUTRITIONAL INFO

PER FLAPJACK (IF MAKING 12) KCAL **265** | FAT **12G** | SATURATES **7G** | CARBS **34G** | SUGARS **17G** | FIBRE **2G** | PROTEIN **3G** | SALT **0.3G**

✳ V

Prep: 25 mins
Cook: 27–35 mins

Best-Ever Chocolate Brownies

Makes 16 squares or 32 triangles

185g (6½oz) unsalted butter, cut into cubes

185g (6½oz) dark chocolate (at least 70% cocoa solids)

85g (3oz) plain flour

40g (1½oz) cocoa powder

3 large eggs

275g (9¾oz) golden caster sugar

50g (1¾oz) white chocolate, chopped into chunks

50g (1¾oz) milk chocolate, chopped into chunks

NUTRITIONAL INFO

PER TRIANGLE (IF MAKING 32) KCAL **150** | FAT **9G** | SATURATES **5G** | CARBS **15G** | SUGARS **12G** | FIBRE **1G** | PROTEIN **2G** | SALT **0.1G**

1 Tip the butter cubes into a medium heatproof bowl. Break the dark chocolate into small pieces and drop into the bowl. Fill a small saucepan about a quarter full with hot water, then sit the bowl on top so that it rests on the rim of the pan, not touching the water. Put over a low heat until the butter and chocolate have melted, stirring occasionally to mix them. Remove the bowl from the pan. Alternatively, cover the bowl loosely with cling film and put in the microwave for 2 minutes on full power. Leave the melted mixture to cool to room temperature.

2 While you wait for the chocolate to cool, heat the oven to 180°C/160°C fan/350°F/Gas Mark 4. Line the base of a shallow 20cm (8 inch) square baking tin with foil or baking parchment.

3 Tip the flour and cocoa powder into a sieve held over a medium bowl. Tap and shake the sieve so that they run through together and you get rid of any lumps.

4 Break the eggs into a large bowl and tip in the sugar. With an electric mixer on maximum speed, whisk the eggs and sugar together for 3–8 mins until the mixture looks thick, creamy and pale and is about double its original volume. Lift out the beaters and wiggle them from side to side. If the mixture that runs off the beaters leaves a trail on the surface of the mixture in the bowl for a second or two, it's ready.

5 Pour the cooled chocolate mixture over the eggy mousse, then gently fold together with a rubber spatula in a figure of eight, being careful not to knock out the air. Move the bowl round after each folding so that you can get at it from all sides until the two mixtures are combined and the colour is a mottled dark brown.

6 Hold the sieve over the bowl of chocolate mixture and resift the cocoa and flour mixture, shaking the sieve from side to side, to cover the top evenly. Gently fold in using the same figure of eight action as before. The mixture will look dry and dusty at first, but if you keep going gently and patiently, it will end up looking fudgy. Stop just before you feel you should, as you don't want to overdo the mixing.

7 Finally, stir in the white and milk chocolate chunks until they're dotted throughout. Pour the mixture into the lined tin, scraping every bit out of the bowl with the spatula. Gently ease the mixture into the corners of the tin and level it across the top.

8 Bake for 25 mins, then pull out the oven shelf and gently shake the tin. If the brownie wobbles in the middle, it's not quite done, so slide it back in and bake for another 5 mins until the top has a shiny, papery crust and the sides are just beginning to come away from the tin. Remove from the oven.

9 Leave the brownie in the tin until completely cold, then lift it out with the foil or parchment. Cut into quarters, then cut each quarter into four squares and finally into triangles, if you like. The brownies will keep in an airtight container for a good two weeks and in the freezer for up to a month. Defrost fully at room temperature before eating.

Index

Index

UK/US Glossary

aubergine – eggplant

bacon lardons – matchsticks of slab bacon

baking parchment – wax paper/parchment paper

baking tray – baking sheet

beetroot – beets

bicarbonate of soda – baking soda

butter beans – lima beans

caster sugar – superfine sugar

cavolo nero – Tuscan kale

chickpeas – garbanzo beans

chilli flakes – red pepper flakes

chips – French fries

chopping board – cutting board

cider – hard cider

cling film – plastic wrap

cocktail stick – toothpick

coriander (fresh) – cilantro

cornflour – cornstarch

courgette – zucchini

dark muscovado sugar – if unavailable, use regular dark brown sugar

demerara sugar – raw or turbinado sugar

dessicated coconut – if unavailable, use unsweetened shredded coconut

double cream – heavy cream

flaked almonds – sliced almonds

foil – aluminium foil

frying pan – skillet

griddle pan – grill pan

grill – broil/broiler

hob – stove

icing sugar – confectioners' sugar

King Edward potatoes – if unavailable, use Russet potatoes

king prawn – jumbo shrimp

light muscovado sugar – if unavailable, use regular light brown sugar

Maris Piper potatoes – if unavailable, use Russet or Yukon Gold potatoes

minced – ground

natural yogurt – plain yogurt

pak choi – bok choy

peppers (green/red/yellow) – bell peppers

plain flour – all-purpose flour

prawn – shrimp

rapeseed oil – canola oil

roasting tray – roasting pan

rocket – arugula

self-raising flour – self-rising flour

semi-skimmed milk – reduced-fat milk

sieve – fine-mesh strainer

single cream – light cream

soured cream – sour cream

spring onions – green onions/scallions

stock – broth

sultanas – golden raisins

sweetcorn – corn

tea towel – dish towel

tomato purée – tomato paste